W9-CPC-353

ADVENTURES IN WATERCOLOR PAINTING

Adventures

IN WATERCOLOR PAINTING

by Paul Montgomery

McGRAW-HILL BOOK COMPANY, INC.

New York Toronto London

ADVENTURES IN WATERCOLOR PAINTING

Library of Congress Catalog Card Number: 54-8101

Published by the McGraw-Hill Book Company, Inc.
Printed in the United States of America

To Frances

PREFACE

In a very real sense this book is an introduction to watercolor painting, but that would be too formidable a title for so simple and informal a treatment of the subject. It is designed for persons who are toying with the idea of taking up watercolor painting as a hobby, or who have decided to do so but don't quite know how to begin.

For an amateur artist who paints watercolors purely as a hobby to write a book about watercolor painting is, at first thought, appallingly presumptuous. That was my own reaction when the idea was first suggested to me. But I found myself rather easily persuaded that the idea had merit. Perhaps that was because it is flattering to be invited to write a book. Who hasn't felt the urge at some time in his life? But also, as I gave the matter mature thought, it seemed to me that this was the kind of book an amateur should write and that maybe I was the amateur who could do it.

I believe I understand the urges and inhibitions of those who consider the possibilities of watercolor painting as a hobby. I have been through the whole experience myself. Perhaps at the very beginning they will find the suggestions of a venturesome amateur more helpful than the instructions of a professional artist or teacher. Possibly their concepts of the personal appeal of this hobby to them will be shaped more effectively by an understanding amateur than by a recognized authority.

That is my only excuse for writing this book. I hope as you read it you will not feel I have become pedantic. I have no right to be. I have only tried to share with others my enthusiasm for a hobby which has provided me with endless hours of absorbing and satisfying relaxation and a whole range of new and heart-warming interests. I have tried to tell as simply as possible how to get started in watercolor painting, how to acquire an understanding of a few essentials. And I have leavened the loaf of practical instruction with incidents from my personal experience which illustrate the solution of elementary problems and the adventures which go hand in hand with the pursuit of this delightful hobby.

There is nothing formidable or forbidding about watercolor painting. It is fun—pure, unadulterated, absorbing, relaxing, challenging fun.

Paul Montgomery

CONTENTS

chapter 1 WATERCOLOR PAINTING AS A HOBBY

Sooner or later nearly everyone feels the need of a hobby—an engrossing interest to which he can turn in his spare time and in which he can find deep satisfaction, effortless relaxation, and complete escape from the tensions of life. This is as true of women who have spent their days handling the involved but repetitive routines of homemaking as it is of men in business and the professions.

Golf, tennis, bridge, and canasta are all good pastimes. They have a place in the scheme of things, but they fail to gratify an urge for that creative self-expression which one finds so deeply satisfying in an ideal hobby. This, I believe, is one reason why pastimes alone do not meet one's needs.

Wherever I turn these days, I find an increasing interest in hobbies. Women devote fewer and fewer hours to cooking and housekeeping duties now that a greater range of automatic appliances is readily available. Men have more leisure time on their hands because of a shorter work week and longer vacations. And each year more men in business face the implications of compulsory retirement at an age when they are still mentally alert and physically active.

But neither the tensions of business nor the implications of retirement led to my interest in watercolor painting as a hobby. At a time when I was still playing golf and tennis with zest and enjoyment, something sparked my interest in painting. Perhaps it was because I had never been an outstanding performer in sports that I began to feel a desire for an avocation which would require something other than muscle. Maybe it was because of a subconscious urge for some form of self-expression. At any rate, propinquity to a small summer art school during my vacations did the rest.

Watercolor painting has been my hobby now for twelve years or more. No other pastime has ever enriched my life so much or proved so satisfying in so many different ways. For watercolor painting not only has provided an outlet for creative effort but has opened up to me a whole new range of interests, the appeal of which I would never have been aware of had I not been exposed to them through the medium of my favorite hobby. The by-products of this happy avocation have been as varied, as heart-warming, and as valuable as its direct benefits in personal satisfactions.

Watercolor painting is an effortlessly absorbing hobby. Once you start the pencil outline of a watercolor subject, everything else fades out of your mind. You become so deeply engrossed in your undertaking that you are unaware of the passing of time. You are oblivious to your surroundings and, for the most part, to the persons who tiptoe up behind you to peer over your shoulders. Painting is something on which I've never had to force myself to concentrate. I have compared my experience with that of other amateurs, and their comments convince me that my experience is universal.

That quality of effortless absorption is something I have rarely experienced with any other pastime. I have always read a great deal, but not always effortlessly. For many years I played both golf and tennis, but never with the easy, relaxed absorption I have experienced in painting. Since I was never an outstanding player, time never passed so quickly for me on the golf course or the tennis court as it does while I am painting a watercolor. Three hours —about my average on the scene in doing a watercolor—are gone before I know it.

There was a time when I went through my daily life rather unaware of the color and the beauty in things around me. It took something pretty spectacular to make a dent on my consciousness. Now I am acutely conscious of color in everything I see, and I see pictures wherever I turn. Only when you begin to paint do you become aware of how much form and color there are in nature and in the structures which are the products of human hands. Things you have passed again and again in your normal routine begin to look more interesting and more colorful, and you see challenging material for pictures in subjects which once seemed drab, dilapidated, and uninteresting.

Watercolor painting as a hobby has made still another contribution to my life. My own efforts as an amateur aroused my interest in the works of professionals. I began to visit the one-man shows of topflight watercolorists in the commercial galleries in New York and other cities and the group shows in the public art galleries and to spend hours at each annual show of the American Watercolor Society in the National Academy School of Fine Arts in New York. From the very first my own struggles have helped me to appreciate the skills of outstanding watercolorists and the artistry of their accomplishments.

My hobby, therefore, opened up a whole new world which I had scarcely been aware of and which I now find intensely interesting.

In a modest way I have become a collector. As a result of these visits to art shows, my admiration for the work of truly accomplished artists, and my inability to resist temptation, I have become the owner of a few highly prized examples of the work of some of our best watercolorists. And when I could not afford to buy originals, I acquired a few fine reproductions.

Another appealing by-product of my favorite

EROS
PAUL MONTGOMERY '54

Cargo for the EROS

Waterfront scenes offer colorful subjects and characteristic problems. Note the water mirrors closely the color of the sky. Shadows and reflections are handled casually to give the effect of water in slight movement.

hobby is the adventures in human contacts I experience while painting in the open. If you doubt that the world is full of gentle, friendly people, all you have to do is get out and paint. Nearly every time I pick a spot and start a watercolor, someone comes along, stops to see what I am doing, and engages in conversation. The number of people, ranging from school children to octogenarians, who are vicariously interested in art never ceases to amaze me. The deference and consideration they show toward an artist at work—with the occasional exception of children who sometimes crowd too close for comfort in their eagerness to see what goes on—is heartwarming. And even among the children there are usually thoughtful youngsters who voluntarily take command of their contemporaries if they get in the way or if there is too much pushing and scuffling as they lose interest in the show.

I always feel, as I become conscious that someone is watching me work, that I should explain I'm only an amateur—that painting is just a hobby of mine and that they are not witnessing the creation of a masterpiece. Such disclaimers usually bring protests that I may not be a professional but what I'm doing is wonderful. The public—at least my public—is almost without exception generous and uncritical. I rarely hear a critical word and never an unkind one from any of them.

A common interest in painting as a hobby, discovered in casual conversation with new acquaintances, always brings a quick and warm response. There is a contagious enthusiasm among amateurs and a spontaneous interest in each other's work and experiences that make for ready understanding and engaging relationships.

One of the many advantages of watercolor painting as a hobby is the fact that it doesn't involve great physical effort; it imposes no strain on your heart. You can indulge in it long, long after your physician has told you to stop playing squash, or tennis, or golf. It's good for the rest of your life.

And it's inexpensive. You don't have to belong to a club. There are no initiation fees or dues. Once you have bought your original equipment you can buy all the materials and supplies you can use in a year of active week-end painting for less than the cost of the greens fees, caddies' fees, golf balls, and drinks involved in one afternoon of golf.

If you look forward to eventual retirement—compulsory or otherwise—on a reduced income, you can be confident that here is one hobby which will fit into your budget for a new way of life. I am convinced that it will do much to enrich that new way of life and that it is a hobby that will bring you satisfaction and tranquility.

Most of the things I have said about watercolor painting as a hobby could no doubt be said about painting with other media. I am not in a position to say. I've had such fun with watercolors and have found them so endlessly challenging that I've never been tempted to try any other medium.

You will hear people say that watercolor painting

is difficult to learn. Frankly, I feel the difficulties have been exaggerated. As a result, many an amateur who might have had great fun with watercolors has been frightened away from the medium and has started with oils—if he has started at all.

Whether one will find painting watercolors or oils the more satisfying hobby is at least partly a matter of personal temperament. One works relatively fast in watercolors—much faster than in oils—and in the main less meticulously. Depending on how complex the subject may be and how big the paper he is using, an amateur watercolorist can do a picture in from one to three or four hours. If done in oils, the same subject in equally competent hands would take at least most of a day and might run to several days. No two artists work with the same degree of speed and precision in any medium, but the point I am making is that oils are inherently the slower and, for most people, the more meticulous medium.

In choosing between watercolors and oils, the amateur should take into consideration his own temperament and work habits as measured against those of the medium. Has he the patience to work with oils, to come back to the same subject again and again in order, after a series of protracted struggles, to achieve his final result? If, on the other hand, he prefers to work at a fairly lively pace and achieve a final result rather quickly, watercolors are his dish.

The amount of time one normally has free to devote to one's hobby also should have something to do with one's choice of medium. Most of us who are not men and women of leisure have only a limited amount of time at our disposal. I can accomplish more in that time by working in watercolors. Furthermore, I find it more satisfying to have a result —good or bad—at the end of a precious two or three hours than to have only a beginning, a partial result which must be added to piecemeal as I can find the necessary time at some later date.

Beginning and ending a painting expedition are much more complicated for the oil painter, from my observation, than for the watercolorist. Contrast the simplicity of rinsing a paint tray and two or three brushes with water and the complications involved in cleaning an oil palette, palette knife, and brushes with turpentine. Contrast the nuisance and the smell, if nothing else!

The argument advanced for oils as a medium for beginners is that one can correct mistakes in oils but not in watercolors. The statement in regard to watercolors is only partly true. Some mistakes can be corrected in watercolors—by sponging out areas or by surpainting lighter colors with dark—but the relatively low cost of watercolor paper and paints makes it possible to begin over again and still not be extravagant if a sketch becomes irretrievable. No matter what medium he uses, every amateur will make some false starts and waste some materials.

Looking back over my twelve years of experience as an amateur watercolorist, I can truthfully say that I have never once regretted my choice of water-color painting as a hobby. My only regret is that I didn't start sooner. If the relaxed and carefree hours I have spent painting during that time haven't added years to my life, they have at least enriched the years I have lived.

What this hobby can mean to a man who has worked hard all his life and who is at a point in his career where he carries heavy and compelling business responsibilities is difficult to appraise or describe —or, for that matter, what it can mean to anyone who feels the need of complete relaxation and an absorbing interest.

How can he describe the ease with which he sheds his problems and concerns as he becomes engrossed in the possibilities of an appealing subject? How can he interpret the thrill of seeing a picture assume form and color under his own hands? How can he help others understand the rich satisfaction he finds in this form of self-expression, the quiet joy of creative accomplishment? These are things we learn only from our own experience.

It is my earnest hope, however, that I have done sufficient justice to my subject to persuade you that painting should be your hobby, too, and water-colors your medium. If you succumb to my persuasion and your experience proves comparable to my own, you have many happy, relaxed, and thoroughly enjoyable hours ahead of you.

You are on the threshold of a wonderful hobby.

chapter 2 GETTING STARTED

In the village far out on the South Shore of Long Island where my family and I have spent most of our summer holidays for nearly twenty years, there was, before World War II, a summer art school. It was housed in a charming little early-colonial dwelling to one side of which a studio wing had been added, and it was located in the center of the village just across the street from the post office. As a result, no one who spent any time at all in that general vicinity could be unaware of its existence.

I found myself mildly curious about what went on inside—or outside, for I often saw student groups starting out on painting expeditions—but my days were quite full—golf and tennis, surf bathing, sunning on the beach, the lazy hours of reading, and the normal but simple social activities that go with that kind of environment. Several summers passed before I found my curiosity piqued to the point of action.

Just what finally got me off dead center, I am not sure I know. Back in my high-school days in a small Middle Western city I had had the usual involuntary exposure to art classes. I suppose I learned a few fundamentals of drawing, and I remember doing a few watercolors of still-life subjects. All our painting was done in the classroom.

At some time during that experience one of my watercolors was hung, along with the work of many others, in an exhibition of the accomplishments of the art class, and—if my memory isn't too glowing —I believe my still life received an honorable mention. Whatever mild thrill of pleasure I experienced at that recognition passed off very quickly, and, my compulsory art training completed, I turned my attention to other things.

The thought of pursuing a career in art never occurred to me. In the corn belt in those days very few people ever thought of art as a way of making a living. As far as I knew at that time only those undertook it whose talents bordered on genius or whose private income enabled them to live the life of a dilettante. At any rate I went on through high school and college and into business without so much as a passing thought that full-time devotion to art might be something I should consider as a way of life.

I have no regrets as I look back on the path I followed. I am convinced that my talents were too modest to justify the choice of art as a career, or as a livelihood. When I rediscovered art as an interest, it took its logical place in my life as a deeply satisfying and absorbing avocation—a gratifying means of self-expression. It is in that area that creative art really belongs in the lives of most of us. We want to master our techniques as best we can in order to express ourselves well when we put color on paper in our interpretation of what we see around us—just as we like to master the English language in order to express our thoughts in conversation or in correspondence. The fact that we cannot create great masterpieces of art should be no more frustrating or discouraging to us than our inability to write great books. Our pictures will bring pleasure to our friends—and ourselves—just as we hope our conversation and our letters bring pleasure.

But to get back to my story, my mild curiosity about the art school must have stirred something in my subconscious, for after eying the school from a distance for two or three summers I began to wonder whether I could nerve myself to go in and ask about it.

My wife was driving me to the station to catch the early-morning train to the city one Monday morning—I stayed in town during the week and made the three-hour trip to the shore only for week ends—when, as we passed the summer art school, I could contain my curiosity no longer.

"Darling," I began tentatively, "would you do me a great favor?"

"What?"

"Stop in at the summer art school sometime this week and ask if they ever take pupils of other than school ages."

"Don't tell me you are thinking about taking up art!" she exclaimed in astonishment.

"Well," I went on hesitantly, "I begin my vacation next week and I just thought maybe . . . well, anyway, stop in and ask them. I might join a class during my vacation."

When I got off the train the following Friday evening, my wife was bubbling with news. Halfway through her report of the developments of the week she plunged into the subject of the art school.

"They tell me," said she, "that they have pupils of all ages from sixteen to sixty and they'll be glad to have you enter. The landscape class goes out three mornings a week—Mondays, Wednesdays, and Fridays—from nine o'clock to twelve. They have a little shop in the school and you can buy all the supplies you need right there."

That settled it. The following Monday morning I reported to the summer art school and began the experience which has come to mean so much to me.

You may well ask at this point, "Why, if you believe this book can be helpful to other amateurs, did you join an art class and seek formal training for yourself?" To which my answer is: "I believe in using every method and device which is readily available for hastening one's progress." I have had time for only a limited amount of formal training in classes under the supervision of a professional artist, and I have found both books and magazines dealing with watercolor painting invaluable as a supplement to that formal training.

I have never understood persons who took up painting as a hobby and decided to go it alone without help from anyone. There may be some psychological satisfaction in being self-taught, but a terrific amount of time is wasted in learning by tedious trial and error what can be learned quickly in a few easy and inexpensive lessons.

At the time I took up watercolor painting as a hobby, two-week vacations were relatively standard. Mine was no exception. The maximum number of lessons I could get in, therefore, was six in a two-week period. But it usually managed to rain at least one or two of the days the landscape class was scheduled to fare forth, and as a result I averaged only four or five lessons a summer for two or three years. Then along came World War II, and the summer art school closed. Since then, with the exception of one winter during which I attended art classes quite regularly (approximately once a week), I have been on my own, but always supplementing my personal experience by studying the techniques of others.

I try to attend the important watercolor shows to see the work of the best professionals. I subscribe to a magazine which each month reproduces in color a picture done by an outstanding watercolorist and in an accompanying article—usually in the form of a personal statement from the artist—describes the colors which comprise his palette, the weight and the type of paper he uses, his selection of brushes, and his procedures in painting a watercolor.

And finally I read books. There are a number of fine books, most of which prove most helpful when one has mastered the elementary phases of watercolor painting.

Yes, I believe in learning from others by any or all the means which are readily available. But at the same time let me add one word of caution: don't become so dependent on a teacher or the comforting presence of other struggling artists in class groups that you fail to strike out boldly by yourself. No amount of training will ever be a substitute for practice, for the experience you gain on your own. My advice is to get out and paint.

That admonition, however, presupposes the command of a few fundamentals; for one thing, the ability to make a simple outline drawing. For in painting a watercolor one starts by drawing the outlines of the various elements in the picture and then fills them in with color. What I am describing here is the simplest kind of freehand drawing, outlining the shape of trees and shrubs, houses and barns, windows and doors, paths and roadways, in the relationship to each other which you want them to have in your picture. But your outline sketch must be drawn in fairly accurate perspective.

The ability to achieve perspective is a fundamental you must learn at the very beginning of your experience with this new hobby. It is neither difficult nor forbidding. It is through the achievement of perspective that you succeed in reproducing on a flat surface—your watercolor paper—natural objects as they appear in the scene you have chosen as your subject.

You accomplish this first in the linear construction of your picture and second in the use of light and shade, intensity of color, and varying degrees of sharpness of detail in the process of painting your watercolor.

Let's take the linear construction first. All lines in any scene have a tendency to converge as they go away from you. Take the simplest traditional example, a railroad track. If you stand squarely between the rails of a straight stretch of railroad track, you will see that the rails seem to converge as your eyes follow them into the distance.

This seeming convergence is true of all lines. If there are telegraph lines along the railroad right of way, you will notice that the poles seem to grow shorter and shorter as they fade into the distance.

Here are three illustrations of the way lines in a pencil sketch must be made to converge in order to give true perspective. All parallel lines seem to converge as they move toward the horizon or vanishing point. This has the effect of making the railway roadbed grow narrower and the telegraph poles shorter as they approach the horizon. Note the convergence also in the roof and foundation lines of the building.

In achieving good perspective in an outline drawing, you will find it helpful to hold your pencil horizontally before your eyes. The angle of the lines in your subject becomes apparent immediately. Angles from the perpendicular can be determined easily by holding your pencil in a vertical position. What otherwise looks like a difficult problem in freehand drawing becomes relatively easy when you follow this simple practice.

Imaginary lines along the top and bottom of the poles seem to converge as they approach the horizon or vanishing point.

Roof lines and foundation lines of buildings converge as their walls carry increasing distances from you. And even the vertical lines of unusually tall buildings will converge as they rise from you.

You must learn to watch for this convergence, which is to be found in almost every type of drawing you make, and to transfer it to your pencil sketch. In determining the correct direction and convergence of lines in my subject, I frequently hold up my pencil horizontally at arm's length before my eyes. The relationship of the horizontal line of my pencil to the line I'm trying to draw becomes obvious. Carrying that relationship in my mind's eye, I then draw the line on paper, keeping the relationship to the horizontal margins of my sketch pad or watercolor block.

Lines which are below the level of your eye will rise to converge with descending lines above your eye level. Lines exactly at eye level will be practically horizontal as they go away from you toward the vanishing point.

It is necessary to watch for this convergence not only in the general structural lines of buildings but in some of the details as well. For example, a row of windows along the side of a building, if you are looking at the building from an angle, will grow smaller the farther they are away from you. The top and bottom lines of these windows will converge.

Note that the windows will appear to be narrower too, the farther they are away, until they are mere slits in the wall.

This business of holding up a pencil, vertically or horizontally, to determine the direction—the angles from vertical or horizontal—of the lines which are part of the structure of your picture is invaluable to amateurs. It solves many problems in perspective which can otherwise be baffling to the inexperienced artist. It helps in another way, too—namely, in measuring the elements in your subject. Is the structure you are sketching wider than it is tall? Hold up your pencil and measure it horizontally and vertically. Then draw your sketch in the same proportions.

If you are taking up watercolor painting without any previous experience in drawing, you will find it worthwhile to get out in the open and do a number of pencil outline drawings, putting into practice the things we have discussed here in regard to perspective. In a sense it is like spending time on the practice tee before playing your first game of golf. It may seem a serious approach to what one undertakes for fun, but it will pay off.

And one can make practice sketches indoors, too, from snapshots or pictures in newspapers and magazines. The knack of making freehand outline drawings which correctly achieve perspective will come quite rapidly. It is not an impossible task for anyone.

I emphasize the "freehand" because you should not use a ruler. The moment you begin to use a ruler or some other type of straightedge tool, you begin to lose some of the nice casual quality of your drawing and hence, when the painting is finished, of your watercolor as well.

The second method of achieving perspective, as I have said, is in the use of light and shade, intensity of color, and sharpness of detail. The limitations of human sight are such that we see things in relatively sharp detail when they are close to us; we lose that detail when they are farther away. For the most part we see colors more vividly when they are close at hand; we find they become softer the farther they are removed from us. At great distances, trees and mountains of many different shades of color fade out into soft gray-blues. Shadows in the foreground or middle distance add to the feeling of depth. A dark tree or line of woods in the middle distance behind a lighter structure has a tendency to move the structure toward you.

All these effects, used in combination with the converging lines already mentioned, will give depth and perspective to a picture. Sacrifice detail in those areas of your picture to which you want to give a feeling of depth or distance; accentuate detail in foreground material. Don't give everything in your watercolor the same values, the same strength, the same vividness of color.

With practice you will find you can reproduce natural objects on a flat surface and make them look as they appear in the scene you are painting.

chapter 3 WHAT TO START WITH

The equipment you need for starting to paint watercolors is relatively simple and, compared with what is required for most sports, relatively inexpensive.

For example, you need no special costume. Any old clothes that are suitable for the climate will do. Leave smocks to the oil painters and, unless you are a born exhibitionist, don't be tempted to buy a beret.

Your minimum equipment will include the following:

- 2 brushes
- 13 tubes of watercolor paints
- 1 paintbox
- 1 finder, or viewer
- 1 block of watercolor paper
- 1 sketch pad
- 3 pencils
- 1 artgum eraser
- 1 knife
- 1 small sponge
- 1 package of Kleenex
- 1 water bottle and glass
- 1 small handbag

The things I have listed are essentials. There are other items you will want to add as you go along, such as an extra brush or two of different sizes and shapes, a bottle of masking fluid, a campstool or two, perhaps a sun umbrella, and an easel. And at home you will want to have at least one white mat, the opening cut to fit your watercolor block.

Let's discuss each of our items of equipment briefly. It is my own theory that our essential materials and equipment should be of good quality. Let's not add to the difficulties we face as beginners by trying to use materials which impose unnecessary handicaps.

One of your more expensive items will be your brushes. I suggest starting with two. One No. 8 round-pointed red-sable watercolor brush. It will cost approximately $7.50. This type and shape of brush will be one of the most useful in your kit, for you can do almost anything with it from applying washes to painting relatively delicate lines and details, for it can be brought down to a fine point for detail work.

The second brush I would suggest is a flat red-sable ¾ inch wide. This is a brush which also has a multiplicity of uses. It is fine for painting skies or spreading washes over large areas. It will cost approximately $6.

It would be difficult to get along with less than thirteen tubes of watercolors. Let me emphasize the fact that you should buy tubes of watercolors rather than a watercolor box already equipped with little squares of dry colors. The colors which come in tubes can be squeezed into your paintbox in the quantity you want. They will stay fresher, remain easier to use, and result in richer, stronger colors in your pictures than can possibly be achieved by using squares or cakes of paint. Leave the little cakes for kindergarten children.

Your choice of watercolor tubes can be from the lines of any one of several well-known makers, domestic or foreign. Your selection should include one tube of each of the following colors:

Cadmium Red
Alizarin Crimson
Burnt Sienna
Burnt Umber
Cadmium Yellow
Yellow Ocher
Hooker's Green Light
Hooker's Green Dark
French Ultramarine Blue
Cobalt Blue
Cerulean Blue
Payne's Gray
Lampblack

You will discover that these are only a few of the colors which are available to you, and you may be

Equipment. Upper left: Block of watercolor paper on which rest a water bottle, tumbler, pocketknife, fine-texture sponge, and two brushes. Lower left: Watercolor box and mixing pan, and a finder, or viewer. Upper right: Small handbag to carry all equipment (except watercolor block and sketch pad), package of Kleenex. Lower right: All-purpose sketch pad, three pencils (soft, medium, and hard) and artgum eraser.

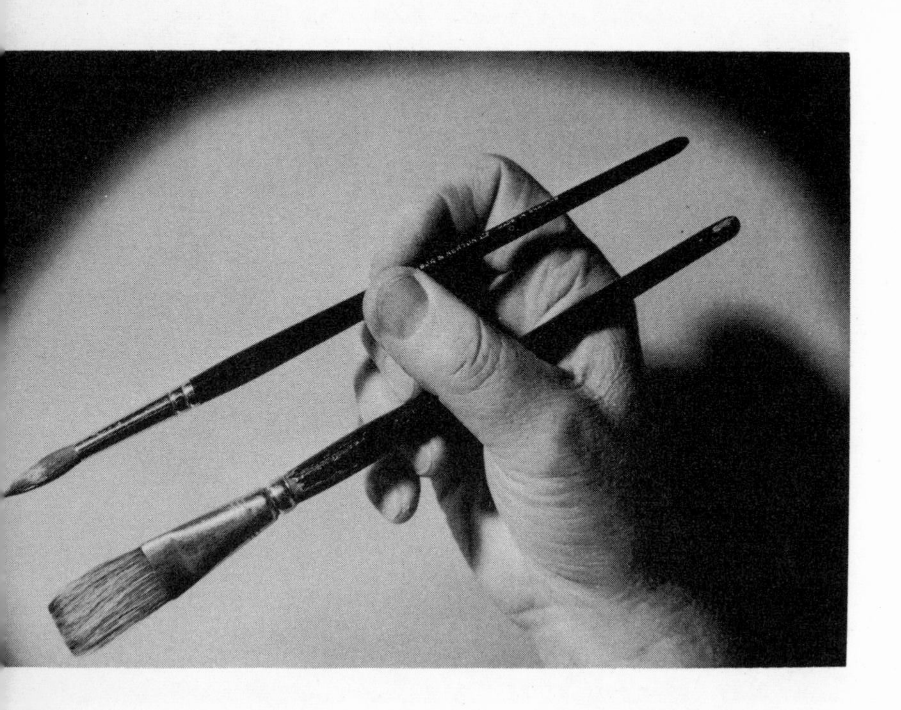

Watercolor brushes. It is desirable to start with two. One should be round and pointed, the other flat. The brushes illustrated are, from top to bottom, a No. 8 round-pointed red-sable watercolor brush and a ¾-inch flat red-sable brush.

tempted to buy many more. I advise against doing so at the beginning. By mixing these colors you can get a wide range of effects. To begin with, any additional tubes are likely to be confusing. Add them to your palette later as you gain experience and begin to see a real need for them.

You may wonder why I have not suggested the purchase of a tube of white watercolor paint. The reason is that you can get the desired result by not painting over the areas you want to appear white in your finished picture. White can be had, and some artists use it sparingly; but most watercolorists let the paper do the work. Unfortunately, white watercolor paint is not transparent and does not mix well with other colors. I advise against its use, particularly during your early experience.

Watercolors of professional quality—and I would certainly buy these rather than the slightly cheaper student grade—range in price from 35 to 85 cents a tube, depending on the color. The thirteen tubes I have suggested for our palette will average out a cost of about 51 cents a tube, or a total of $6.65.

You will, of course, need a paintbox. There are several different types. They will range in price from $2 or $3 up to $6 or $7 or more. One of the most convenient consists of two sections. The lower and outer section has concave impressions across the bottom designed to hold about fifteen tubes of paint and, lengthwise of the box, a space for two or three brushes. The second section, when folded, slides into place as the cover to the entire paintbox. When unfolded, it has, on one half, little sections into which to squeeze paint and on the other a mixing pan divided into two or three sections. There is a thumb hole in this section so that it can be held in the left hand like a palette. It is normally priced at about $5.50.

This is only one of a variety of paintboxes and mixing pans you will find to choose from. Choose the one that appeals to you most. I would only suggest that you select one which can either be held in your hand or placed on a box or table conveniently near while you are painting. There will be varying circumstances under which you may want to handle your box either way.

A finder, or viewer, is simply a piece of rigid white cardboard of small size—about 6 by 8 inches in outside dimensions—in which is cut an aperture about 4 by 6 inches. Held up before you, it serves to frame the portion of the scene you may want to paint. It helps an artist to "find" the picture for which he is looking.

For a beginner, the choice of a block of watercolor paper is better, I think, than the purchase of individual sheets. The block is easier to handle and is more convenient. If you buy individual sheets, you then have to buy a board or sheet of plywood big enough so that your paper can be mounted upon it. It must be attached by some type of adhesive tape run around the edge of the paper. Thumbtacking is not satisfactory, as the tacks too often get in your way because they stick up slightly above the surface

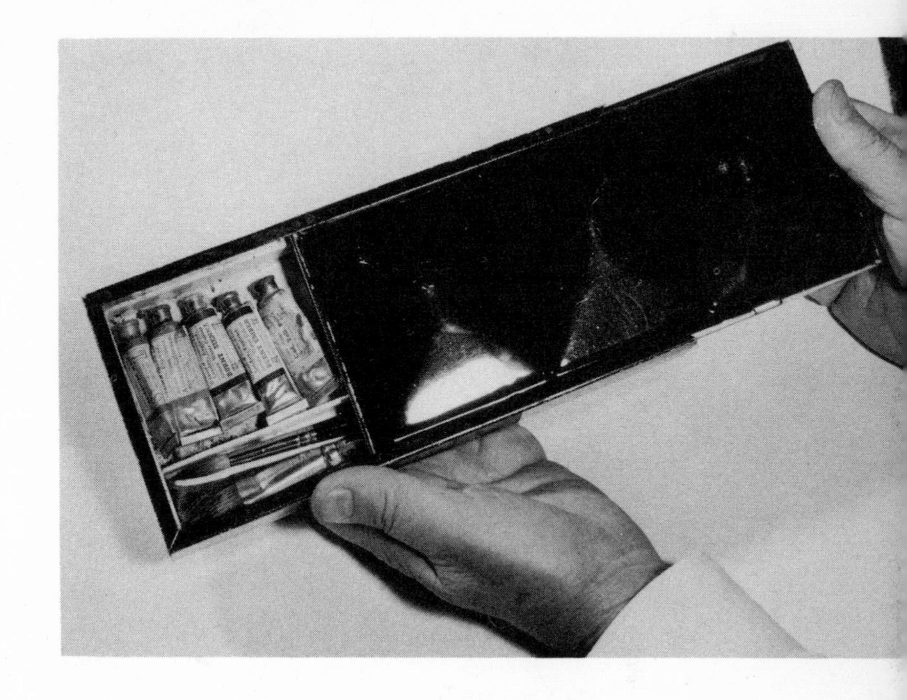

My favorite watercolor box. The lid slides out to reveal watercolor tubes and brushes. The lid itself opens up to provide a palette and mixing pan. The whole unit is compact and easy to handle.

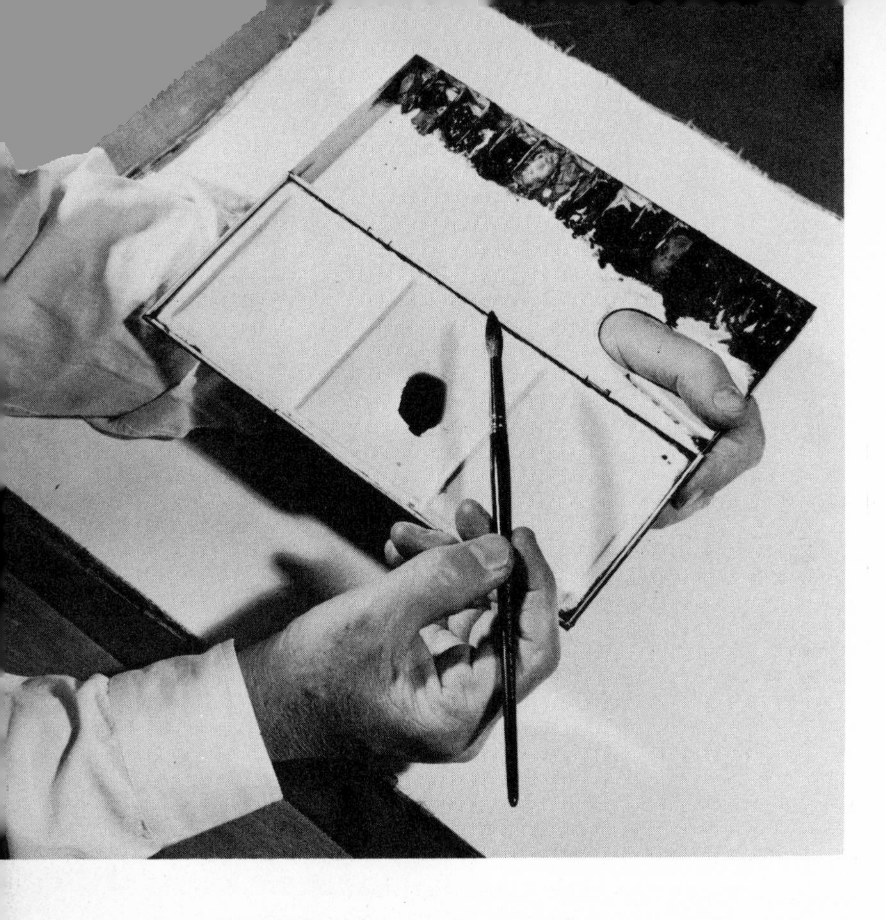

The lid of my watercolor box opened and ready for use. It can either be held in hand as shown here or be laid within easy reach of your right and close to your water glass.

of the board. You have to go through none of these preparations in using a watercolor block. Incidentally, you leave your paper attached to the block until you have completed your picture.

Choose a block of fairly good size. Start with at least 12 by 18 inches or even larger, preferably 16 by 20 inches. For some reason most of us amateurs, left to our own devices, have a tendency to choose small sheets of paper and to make tiny drawings. Perhaps it looks easier but actually it's more difficult. I found a big white sheet of paper a pretty appalling thing when I first started; but one merely draws one's sketch larger and uses bigger brushes and more generous brush strokes than would be possible if one succumbed to the temptation to use a small block. Using the larger paper helps to offset another tendency, the inclination many of us have to overdraw and to be too meticulous in both drawing and painting. Watercolors usually gain in charm by a casual quality in their execution.

Watercolor paper can be purchased in any one of three different surface textures: smooth, medium, and rough. I suggest the selection of a rough paper. Even though you might start with a medium surface, it is almost inevitable that you will come to prefer a rough one sooner or later, for it lends a quality to watercolors which is difficult to obtain on any other surface. The tiny white spots on a rough paper which are accidentally or intentionally left uncovered in the process of painting give a feeling of sparkling light. Most of our professional watercolorists use a rough paper.

As to how heavy a paper to use, I would certainly choose nothing less than a sheet of 140-pound basis weight. You'll find it a practical weight in the sense that it does not ripple or warp seriously when wet. You can apply a rich, juicy wash, and when it dries the paper will still be flat. It is a happy and relatively economical compromise between the lightweight papers, which do ripple easily, and the 240-pound paper, which a professional would use when painting a finished watercolor to enter in an exhibition or put up for sale. The very heavy weights, by the way, can only be bought in sheets instead of in blocks. The 140-pound weight is about as heavy a paper as is available in blocks. The finest of handlaid 140-pound watercolor paper, in blocks of twenty-four sheets measuring 12 by 16 inches, will cost $8. In the 16- by 20-inch size the cost will be about $9.

The sketch pad on our list of essentials can be almost any size. I prefer a 9- by 12-inch spiral-bound pad. The one I use contains twenty-four sheets of a multipurpose paper which is recommended especially for pencil and crayon but is also suitable for pen-and-ink or watercolors.

I use this pad for a variety of purposes. Sometimes I make a preliminary pencil sketch or two of the subject I have chosen, just to shift different elements in the subject in an effort to achieve better

Two simple types of watercolor boxes. The one at left provides generous mixing pans but no storage space for tubes or brushes.

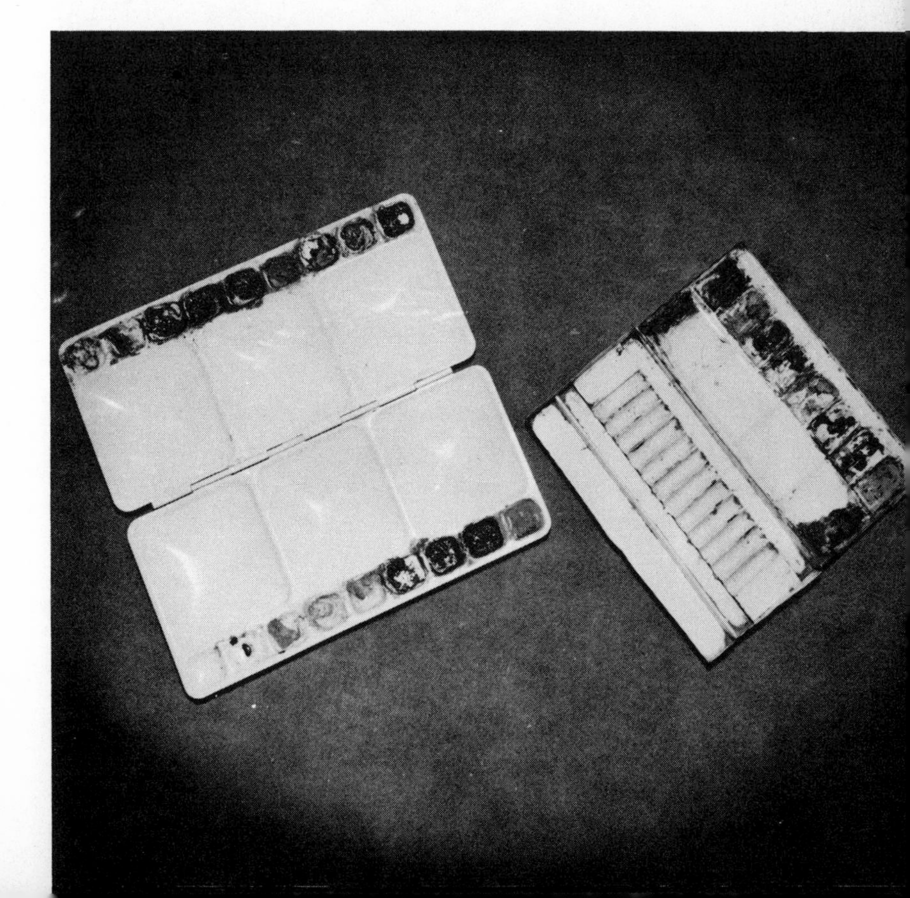

This "viewer," or "finder," is just a bit of cardboard cut to match in miniature the shape of your watercolor block. Held up at varying distances from your eyes, it helps to "find" your picture—to determine how much of the scene you should include in your watercolor.

composition—a better-balanced picture than nature has provided. Sometimes, when weather conditions are unfortunate, or for some other reason I do not want to paint on the spot, I make a pencil sketch with color notes and then do the actual watercolor at home. That is, I write on the margin of the sketch, with arrows pointing to specific areas, or on the areas themselves, notes reminding myself of the colors which I actually saw before me when I was making my pencil sketch.

Still other times—and here is the advantage of a multipurpose paper—I make a quick pencil sketch on the spot and then paint in some color with a few quick brush strokes, thus doing away with the necessity of color notes. And on other occasions, when you are actually doing a watercolor, it is nice to have a pad of clean white paper around on which to test the color you are mixing before applying it to your picture. Such a pad will cost about 35 cents.

The three pencils I suggest, costing about 15 cents each, should give you a range from hard (2-*H*) through medium (*B*) to soft (4-*B*). The artgum eraser is, of course, for use on pencil lines in making your sketches. It will not erase watercolor. It can be had in either of two sizes, at 6 or 12 cents.

Why a knife, and what kind of knife? It has many uses in a watercolor kit. Sharpening pencils is one. A knife with a good sharp-pointed blade also is useful in scratching white lines in dark-colored areas; something you quite frequently have occasion to do, for example, to bring out the halyards of a boat

Morning at the Lobster Dock

A good illustration of the liberties an artist can take in composing and painting a picture. Actually there was no building at the right. It was added merely to enclose the picture and keep the eye from being carried out of it. The structure at the left was white but was painted gray for contrast and to subdue it. The dark shadow in the foreground was added to break up an otherwise uninteresting foreground.

FISH & LOBSTERS

Pencil sketch with color notes. When conditions are not quite right for painting on the scene, or one doesn't have time to do a watercolor, a pencil sketch with color notes will preserve the picture—color and all—for future use. A snapshot of the scene will help too at some future date, but your color notes, which can only be made on a pencil sketch, are important aids when one gets ready to paint.

against a dark background such as a building, a dock, or a background of trees. And then a knife is useful in detaching your finished watercolor from your watercolor block, though you must always be careful not to scratch the surface of the fresh sheet underneath with the point of your knife. A good Boy Scout knife with several blades will serve the purpose as well as any. A small pocketknife is thoroughly practical. Take your choice at $1 to $5.

A small, fine-texture sponge, about three inches in diameter when wet, is a valuable item in your kit. It is useful in moistening a sky area—or any area for that matter—which you plan to paint in rather wet, and it is particularly useful if you become unhappy about an area already painted and want to wash it out. A sponge can be had for 25 to 50 cents.

Kleenex, or a comparable tissue, has many uses. It is a fairly satisfactory substitute for a rag with which to dry your brushes—particularly if you happen to be painting where you cannot flick water or paint from them. It is useful, too, in picking up excess moisture from your paper, or a drop of paint in case of an accident with an oversaturated brush. And it is helpful in softening the edge of a white cloud when blue in the sky would otherwise give it an unnaturally pronounced edge; or in lightening portions of dark clouds or trees by picking up part of the pigment while your paint is still wet. Finally, it is wonderfully useful in cleaning up and drying your mixing pans, paintbox, and brushes as you get ready to pack them up at the end of a morning or afternoon of sketching.

The water bottle and tumbler are obvious essentials. Any old bottle and tumbler or jelly glass you can find around home will do, provided the bottle can be securely capped. I usually carry water with me when I start out to sketch because one cannot always find fresh water conveniently at hand. Carry at least a pint and preferably a quart, for you will want to change your water several times while you are painting. If you don't, you begin to lose clear color values midway in your painting.

And finally, having assembled all this equipment, you face the problem of how to carry it. I use a small canvas zipper bag, into which I cram everything. Mine measures 6 by 12 inches on the bottom and stands about 8 inches high. I picked it up in one of those big chain drug stores that carry everything. My recollection is that it cost about $3. It's a little small, but I like it because I can pack it in a big piece of airplane luggage—a suitcase that is midway between a two-suiter and a trunk locker—which I use if I am taking an extended vacation trip. That big receptacle will even carry my watercolor block laid flat.

The total cost of this minimum stock of equipment will amount to approximately $33. Your watercolor brushes will last for years. I still use the first one I ever bought twelve years ago. Your block of paper will contain twenty-four sheets. Your watercolor tubes contain enough paint to last through the painting of half a dozen to a dozen watercolors. This is true even of the colors you use most. Those you use sparingly seem to last almost indefinitely. The same is true of pencils and erasers—unless you lose them, as I frequently do, and even then they are not costly to replace.

The rest of your equipment is relatively durable, except for Kleenex. Hence the cost of maintaining a modest inventory of supplies is very low. I have never kept an accurate record, but I doubt that I spend an average of $15 a year on supplies. Mind you, I am of course talking only of week-end and vacation painting. And I don't paint every week end. However, I think the amount of painting I do is fairly typical of amateur watercolorists.

Your hobby really begins to run into money when you decide to have your best pictures framed. Even then we are fortunate in the fact that watercolors usually look well in simple frames. And such devices as button-back frames make it possible to substitute one watercolor for another in the frame with the greatest of ease. But that is all another part of the story.

To your list of essential equipment can be added, as you go along, a few extras which contribute to the ease and convenience of painting. A couple of campstools are a good example. They can be picked up at modest cost in hardware or army surplus stores. Although you can usually find a box, a log, or something to sit on while painting—and if worse comes to worst you can always sit on the ground—a campstool is a real convenience, especially to those of us who are no longer so supple as we once were. The extra campstool is useful as a substitute for an easel or, if you have an easel, as a place on which to rest your water receptacle, paint tubes, Kleenex, or other odds and ends which will otherwise be strewn around on the ground.

A collapsible watercolor easel is a great convenience but is not easy to carry around. I never take one with me on a trip unless I am traveling by car and have plenty of room. Do not confuse a watercolor easel with an easel for painting oils. A watercolor easel must have an adjustment which permits your working surface—your paper—to lie almost flat. You want the top of your watercolor block raised slightly, of course, but only 10 or 15 degrees. An oil painter, on the other hand, sets his working surface—his canvas—almost vertical. An easel designed only for oil painting is therefore not suitable for a watercolorist.

A sun umbrella makes it possible to work in places where, without the shade it provides, it would be extremely difficult to do a good watercolor because of the blinding glare of sun on paper and because of the speed with which watercolors dry on warm paper exposed to the sun. I didn't buy a portable sun umbrella until I had been painting for several years in the same area far out on Long Island. When I finally bought it, I found that within a relatively limited area I had a lot of new subjects available, simply because I could now sit where they could be painted and still not be exposed to the sun.

But my advice to my fellow amateurs is to buy only minimum essentials. It is easy to add the conveniences later when you find you have really succumbed to this enthralling hobby.

chapter 4 GETTING READY TO PAINT

Before you start out on your first painting expedition, there are some simple things you will find it desirable to do at home to familiarize yourself with your materials.

Let's start with pencils and paper. If you have followed my suggestions, you have equipped yourself with three drawing pencils ranging from hard to soft in this order: 2-*H, B,* and 4-*B*. You also have a pencil sketch pad in addition to your watercolor block.

You will use your pencils in two ways. First, you will find it helpful on many occasions to make a little preliminary sketch of your subject. You may do this because you want to shift some elements in the scene to produce a more compact or better-balanced picture. Or you may make a pencil sketch to determine what relative values in lights and darks give you the best effect. Second, as we pointed out in an earlier chapter dealing with the subject of perspective, it is almost essential—certainly for an amateur—to draw an outline of the principal components of the final picture before you start laying color on paper. You thus block out with pencil outline the areas which you fill in with color later.

It is worth a little experimenting to see what effects you can get in preliminary composition and value sketches with your soft, medium, and hard pencils. Just as a try, draw the outline of a barn on your pencil sketch pad, using your hard pencil (2-*H*). Shade it on one side with your medium pencil (*B*). Put some trees or a hill behind it, and then decide whether to shade the background very dark and heavy with your soft pencil (4-*B*) or gray and light with your hard pencil (2-*H*).

Use your artgum eraser to make a couple of changes, just to see how it works.

In drawing an outline for a watercolor sketch, you will ultimately have to decide after some experience whether it adds or detracts from your pictures to have your pencil outline show through in the final watercolor. Some of our top-flight watercolorists feel that casually sketched pencil outlines are a desirable element in the finished product. For a beginner, whose sketches may involve many erasures, it's a pretty good idea to make the pencil outline lightly with a medium (*B*) pencil with a view to losing the lines entirely in the finished picture. At any rate, I'd suggest that you try your early

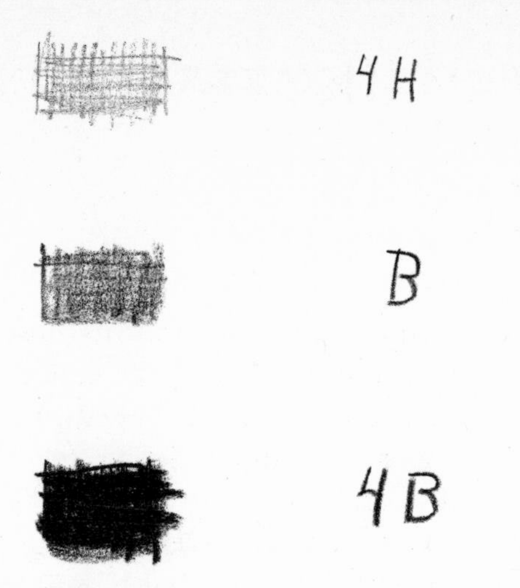

*These crosshatch doodles give an idea of the shading from gray to black you have at your command in 4-*H, B, *and 4-*B *pencils. Two preliminary sketches, illustrating both the uses of hard and soft pencils, in gray and black shading, and two ways of treating the same subject. In one the foreground is kept dark and strong and the background light. In the other the shading is reversed, with the background strong and dark. Either will make a good watercolor as far as color values are concerned. Preliminary sketches like these will frequently help one decide which approach is best for a specific landscape.*

outline sketches with a medium (*B*) pencil, eventually working to a harder or softer pencil as suits your taste.

Now let's try to get the "feel" of our painting materials—our watercolors and brushes. It's a good idea to adopt from the start a standard arrangement of colors in your paintbox. The habit of always squeezing out your paints into the same compartments and in the same order saves time and prevents mistakes when you are in the midst of a rapidly moving watercolor. You will find, as your experience grows, that you acquire something like the touch system in typewriting; that is, you know where to reach for a color without looking all over your box.

I suggest this procedure and arrangement. Place your folding paintbox on a table or desk in front of you, with the paint compartments away from you and the mixing tray toward you. Now take your paint tubes and squeeze about a half inch of paint into each paint compartment, beginning in the left-hand corner and following this order across the paintbox from left to right:

Cadmium Red
Alizarin Crimson
Burnt Sienna
Burnt Umber
Cadmium Yellow
Yellow Ocher
Hooker's Green Light
Hooker's Green Dark
French Ultramarine Blue
Cobalt Blue
Cerulean Blue
Payne's Gray
Lampblack

Now try the colors and see what you get. At last you are ready to take brush in hand and put paint on paper. Set a tumbler of water (about three-quarters full) at your right and within easy reach. Lay your block of watercolor paper before you.

What you are about to do is to put on paper two modest samples of each of your colors in an orderly arrangement so that you can identify them and label them if you wish. You are going to lay one sample on paper with a brush only slightly moistened with water and then dabbed in color. Then lay on another beside the first with a well-saturated brush. The purpose of this is to learn how your colors look when spread on white paper and to show the varying degrees of intensity, or values, which can be achieved in the same color by carrying varying amounts of water in the brush. The experiment will also reveal the fact that watercolors, when applied to white paper, look lighter after they dry than when they are wet.

To carry your experiment with colors further, mix pure pigments with each other. What happens when you mix red with yellow, red with green, or red with blue? Try it and see. A little farther along in this chapter we will devote more attention to the subject of color. You can study the chromatic scale and read a wealth of material on the subject, but the simplest and easiest way to find the answer is to mix them yourself, with your own brush, apply them to paper, and see the result. Yes, you probably already know—if you took any art courses at all in grammar school, high school, or college—that red and yellow will produce orange, red and green will produce brown, and red and blue will produce purple. But most of us amateurs learn by doing; at least we learn more rapidly, and what we learn by doing becomes instinctively part of us rather than an abstract intellectual process.

While you have paints and watercolor block before you, you can make a couple of additional discoveries for yourself that are worth tucking away in your mind for future reference. One of them is that if you lay a moist color over the edge of a color which has already dried on your paper, it will leave a hard edge. Sometimes you want that effect somewhere in a watercolor sketch and at other times you don't. It depends on the subject. The point is to have such command of your materials that you get it when you want it and avoid it when you don't.

For example, if you are painting a house or barn the front of which is in bright sunshine and the side in deep shadow, you want a hard sharp edge at the corner of the structure where bright and shaded sides meet. This is usually achieved after the light side has been painted and has had time to dry. You then lay the darker color of the shaded side along the edge of the light surface, overlapping by a hairline to achieve a sharp hard edge. Shadows cast by overhanging eaves should be surpainted in the same way with a sharp hard edge. A dark roof against a lighter sky is another example.

On the other hand, a house settles comfortably into the lawn around it if the color of the grass is shaded into the color of the foundation to produce a soft edge. A chimney looks less precariously poised on the roof of a house if its base is given a soft rather than hard edge where chimney and roof meet. And a tree looks leafier and more natural if its edges are softened here and there where it meets the sky.

You can create a soft edge by quickly picking up a little of your color with a piece of Kleenex or with a slightly moist—but not saturated—brush.

The other discovery you should make is that if you lay a wet color along the edge of a color which is still moist, capillary attraction will cause the freshly laid color to run or "creep" into the area which is still moist. Try it while you have your materials before you. This characteristic can be put to good use at times if you have command of your materials. You can soften the soft blue or lavender of distant wooded land into hazy outlines against the sky by painting it in swiftly while the sky area at horizon level is still moist. There are even times when an accidental "creep" which you did not intend to induce turns out to be a fortunate accident.

One rainy Saturday morning I parked my car on a side street just off the East River Drive in New York and, sitting in the front seat, went to work on a watercolor. The focal point of attention in the picture was a couple of cylindrical concrete coal-storage bins, topped by a blackened steel superstructure which extended out over the water and from which a big coal bucket was mechanically raised and lowered to hoist finely ground coal from the barges at the water's edge. Gusts of wind occasionally whipped off a black cloud of coal dust as the loaded bucket was raised to the top of the bins.

In planning my watercolor as I sketched in the outline of my subject I had no thought of trying to include this flying coal dust. However, after floating in a wet gray sky and waiting until I thought it was dry, I started to paint in, over the sky, the heavy dark outline of the superstructure with the bucket drawn up immediately beneath it. To my horror I found the sky was still moist and that my pigment was starting to creep rapidly into it. At first I was frantic and was on the point of trying to pick up the fresh color with a piece of Kleenex or a dry brush when I discovered that I was getting the effect of coal dust swept from the bucket by a gust of wind. So I let it alone, except to soften the edge of the creep slightly by touching it with a moist brush. The end result added to the general effect of the picture rather than detracting from it. I couldn't have achieved the effect any better if I had practiced various techniques for weeks.

Accidents, such as the one I have just described, are quite common in watercolor painting. They can frequently be observed, if one looks carefully, in the work of our best watercolorists. While accidents do not always add to the impression one is trying to create in a picture, neither do they always detract from it.

It is this characteristic of watercolors, namely, that under some circumstances they will creep or run, that is one of the arguments used against watercolor painting as a hobby for amateurs. It is my own contention that any amateur, with a modest amount of manual dexterity and a little practice of the kind I have suggested, can gain reasonable command of this medium.

The hazards inherent in the physical characteristics of watercolors merely add to the excitement of watercolor painting. They are like sand traps and bunkers on a golf course. What amateur golfer would find the game a challenging sport if golf courses were all smooth fairway—no rough and no hazards?

Your next experiment should be with washes. Start with a fresh sheet of paper. Elevate the end of your watercolor block which is away from you about three inches by placing a book or two under it. Using your largest brush, mix a generous wash of water and color—any color—in your mixing pan. Saturate your brush in it and, holding the brush almost vertical to your watercolor block, sweep it back and forth across the top of your paper. Saturate your brush in the wash again and, overlapping slightly the area you have already covered, repeat the sweep across the paper. Repeat this operation three or four times until you have come down your paper 4 or 5 inches.

To stop the wash, and yet to avoid letting the ripple of water which forms at the bottom of a wash creep back into the surface you have covered, flick the moisture from your brush, or squeeze it out with a rag, and then run your brush back over the bottom edge. It will pick up the excess wash as you go.

You should achieve in this experiment a smooth, even spread of color with no brush strokes showing and few if any spots, even on rough paper, uncovered by your wash. The trick is to have your brush saturated with the same amount of water and pigment for each brush stroke. The moment you begin to use less or more saturation the strokes of your brush will begin to appear.

Try another wash on the rest of your paper, this time after making washes of two different colors in separate portions of your mixing pan. Start with one wash, blue for example, at the top. Then gradually, as you go down the sheet, begin to introduce a little heavier proportion of the second color each time you resaturate your brush until you finally have the second color only. You will find that, with practice, you can shift smoothly from one color to another through intermediate shades and that if you wish to do so, you can introduce other colors as well.

It isn't desirable to keep up these exercises and experiments to the point of boredom. After all, this is a hobby you have undertaken for fun. But it is a good idea to come back to them occasionally after you have begun painting pictures, for they will help you correct faults and solve problems.

Before you do your first watercolor picture, give a little more thought to the subject of color and the colors you are going to employ in your palette. How do you use them to get the effects you want? How do they react to each other? What do we mean when we talk about warm and cool colors, color values, complementary colors?

We can start with this general statement: Red and yellow are warm colors; blue and green are cool colors. Then we have to remind ourselves that there is a whole range of intermediate shades, some of which we can buy ready-mixed in tubes, if we wish, but any of which we can mix ourselves from the colors I have recommended for our palette. The colors in these intermediate shades in which red and yellow predominate in the admixture are also warm colors, and by the same token those in which blue and green predominate are in the cool range.

To be more specific, here are some of the warm shades: the reds, siennas, umbers, browns, tan, violet, red-violet (as distinguished from blue violet), orange-red, orange, yellow-orange, yellow, and even a yellow-green provided the yellow predominates. And here are some of the cool shades: blue-green, blue-violet, green-yellow. There are both warm and cool shades of gray, depending, of course, on whether we allow our warm colors to predominate in the admixtures which produce our grays or whether we let the colder blues predominate.

Pictures in which we set the general tone in warm colors, colors which are picked up and repeated in various places in our subject, are for the most part more pleasing and more inviting than those in cool colors. We can, of course, deliberately make some scenes more grim and forbidding by the use of cool grays in our skies and other important elements in our composition. When I first started painting, I found many of my pictures were disappointingly cold. I soon discovered that I was using too many greens and blues; that I was failing to recognize the warm yellow-greens and sienna tints in grass, in grain crops, and in shrubs and trees, painting all of them too coldly green. Once I saw what was wrong, it was easy to correct.

Let me remind you here that when we speak of color values, we mean the strength of a color and not its shade or place in the color spectrum. As we have already learned in our first modest experiment, described earlier in this chapter, we can vary the strength, or value, of a color by the amount of pigment versus water we carry in our brush. The more pigment and the less water we use, the greater is the intensity of our color and hence the greater its color value.

When we speak of complementary colors or, as some call them, "opposite" colors, we mean those colors which contrast most strongly with each other. When they are mixed together, complementary colors have a tendency to neutralize each other and to produce something approximating one of the shades of gray. The following are technically among what are considered the truly complementary colors: red and blue-green, yellow-red and blue, yellow and purple-blue, green and red-purple, purple and green-yellow.

The traditional means of illustrating this "opposite" quality of complementary colors and fixing them in the mind in their relationship to each other is the color wheel.

We have not provided for a tube of orange color in our palette. You can get it by mixing a little

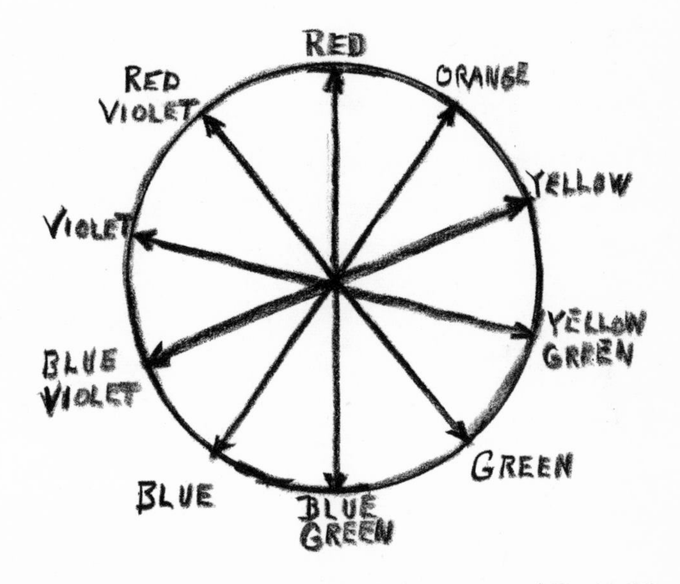

This is the conventional version of the color wheel. Complementary colors are at opposite ends of each line bisecting the circle. Complementary colors, when mixed, have a tendency to neutralize each other.

Alizarin Crimson with Cadmium Yellow. A red-purple can be made by mixing Alizarin Crimson with French Ultramarine Blue, weighting the mix with a predominance of crimson. Purple-blue is made by mixing the same colors but with blue predominating in the mix. The rest of the complementary colors are obvious.

We put this knowledge of complementary colors to good use in toning down colors that would otherwise be too brilliant. For example, we may find in painting a red barn that our Alizarin Crimson is too bright to interpret accurately what we see before us. Mixing a little blue-green with our red will tone it down to the more weather-beaten color we want. In watercolor painting we rarely use pure color just as it comes out of the tube. It is tempered, or neutralized, by the admixture of one or more colors.

No amount of reading on this subject of color will ever take the place of actual practice in mixing colors and applying them to paper. As you can find time to do so, therefore, I urge you to take brush and paint tray in hand and experiment with some of the combinations of colors we have discussed here. You will find that a modest amount of practice will be very rewarding and that soon the ability to get the color you want becomes second nature.

chapter 5 YOUR FIRST WATERCOLOR

Let's assume now that you are ready to do your first watercolor. If the weather is at all favorable, I would suggest that you get outdoors to do it. Getting out in the open is part of the fun of watercolor painting. Still-life pictures, usually done indoors, require more precise techniques in the main than landscapes require. It is better to undertake them after you have had more experience, so I would put them off until later unless, of course, it is midwinter or a rainy day.

What kind of subject should you choose? Anything that appeals to you. But I would recommend that you start with something relatively simple—an old barn or house—of simple lines but nice comfortable proportions and no fancy details.

We amateurs often make the mistake of beginning with subjects that are too complicated for an inexperienced artist. A fellow amateur with whom I was comparing notes one time told me of one of his earliest efforts. He had had a few simple lessons from a professional instructor and then had set out on his own. Without fully realizing what he was doing, he selected a subject which involved a number of trees, buildings, boats, and people. He was pretty badly discouraged by the time he had finished his painting but nevertheless submitted it later to his instructor for criticism. The latter examined it carefully for a moment and then exclaimed, "My God, you amateurs undertake subjects that a Michelangelo would hesitate to tackle!"

I went to the opposite extreme in my own early choice of subject matter. When I first began to paint watercolors, I was spending a vacation out toward the far end of Long Island. A few miles away, at the water's edge, was a little village composed of a fascinating array of shacks and shanties, most of them apparently built of materials salvaged by their owners from a variety of sources. Nestled in low dunes and surrounded by the unkempt gray-green grass that thrives in the sand, they were colorful and picturesque. I did so many of these simple structures that a former golfing companion, who viewed my artistic efforts with a somewhat jaundiced eye, dubbed me "the leading outhouse painter on Long Island."

Since then I've painted everything from ships and bridges to churchyards and cathedrals, but I'm still convinced that it pays to start with simple sub-

jects. We amateurs have so much to learn in handling our materials in our earlier watercolors that we should not complicate our problems by tackling complex subjects.

Having chosen your subject, next pick the exact spot from which to do it. By way of illustration, let's suppose you have picked an old barn with a nice old silo at one end. You must now decide from which angle you want to paint it. Do you want to do it head on, that is, from squarely in front of the barn, as in the first example? Do you want the silo to be the dominant feature in your picture? In that event you will move to one side and your drawing will look like the second example. Or do you want to feature the opposite end of the barn, as in the third example?

What you want to emphasize in your picture obviously dictates the general area in which you pick your spot.

A second thing to consider is the position of the sun. Unless you have a big sun umbrella which you can set up anywhere to protect you and your paper, you will want to pick a spot in the shade. Select a good shady spot under a tree or in the shadow of a building. And be sure the sun will not reach it during the next two or three hours.

The glare of sun on paper is hard on your eyes. Furthermore, it dries your watercolors so fast that it is almost impossible to lay smooth washes or to avoid hard edges.

Having established yourself comfortably, you are

I prefer to paint outdoors when the weather is favorable, but I have painted indoors on many a winter week end. Set up a card table where you have good light but where the sun will not fall directly on your paper. Cover the table with an old cloth, prop up the top of your watercolor block with a couple of books or your kit bag, and you are ready to go to work.

One does not hold a brush close to the point like a pencil. On the contrary it is held well back on the shaft. Resist the temptation to rest your hand or arm on your paper or on the table. If you succumb you will find yourself making little niggling brush strokes instead of wielding your brush boldly and easily.

Watch that glass of water. When it gets as dark as this, it should be changed in order to avoid graying allover colors into dull neutral shades. Crowd yourself to work steadily and rapidly but not to the extent that you unintentionally run one area of paint into another which is still moist.

ready to draw your pencil sketch. At this point take a look at your subject through your finder (or viewer, as some artists call it)—the small white cardboard mat in which you have cut a rectangular opening proportionate to the shape of your watercolor block—and decide how much of the scene you want to include in your picture.

Most of us beginners have a tendency to draw our subjects too small. As a result, if we are to fill our paper, we have to bring in around the subject a lot of material which we really had not intended to include. Draw the subject you have chosen large enough to dominate your picture. Let it cover the bulk of your paper.

Be sure your picture has a focal point of attention, but be careful not to get the focal point of attention squarely in the middle of the picture. In the sketch on page 42 it would be a mistake to place the silo in the center. As a general rule, anything which horizontally or vertically divides a picture into two equal parts creates uncomfortable proportions and bad composition. For this reason, if the horizon is clearly a feature in a landscape or seascape, it should not be placed midway between the top and bottom of your paper. The spire of a church or the mast of a ship should not bisect your paper vertically.

However, in composing our picture we should strive for a sense of balance. This does not mean that we must have the same number and size of trees or buildings in one-half of our picture as we

A well-composed, well-balanced picture is not achieved by placing the focal point of attention squarely in the middle and identical balancing units on each side. In fact, such a picture does not typify good composition. It is uncomfortably bisected rather than balanced.

Good composition, or good balance, can be achieved with the focal point of attention at one side or the other. In this case, a big tree is counterbalanced to some extent by two smaller trees of varying size.

You can place the focal point of attention well in the background of a picture and still achieve good composition, provided you use some device such as a road, fence, or shadow line to help give the eye a path to follow. The thing to guard against is a composition which is completely unbalanced, or one which has no real focal point of attention.

have in the other. That, as a matter of fact, would not make a good composition. It does mean that if we have a big tree on one side of our picture, we will want to consider placing a smaller tree and some shrubs, or a couple of smaller trees, somewhere on the opposite side of the picture. Sometimes this element of balance can be achieved by throwing one side of our foreground in shadow—as if from a tree or building or cloud which does not apear in the picture—in order to offset partly a dominant or heavy object in the other half of our composition. The main point is to give some counterbalance—not necessarily of equal weight—to important and dominant objects which would otherwise completely overweight one side of our picture. A picture can achieve a comfortable feeling of balance with or without equal weight on both sides. Unequal weighting of the balance will usually make the more interesting picture.

Our composition is helped too by a roadway or winding path or other device which subtly helps to carry the eye into the picture, adding to its feeling of depth and perspective.

Once your outline sketch is finished, you complete the rest of your preparations for painting. Squeeze out fresh paint from your tubes, or if you already have an adequate supply in your paint compartments, moisten the paints by running a little water over them, draining it off quickly before they start to run.

In handling your materials you have several choices. You can place your block of paper on an easel, on the ground, or on a box or campstool in front of you, propped up at the top so that washes will flow from top to bottom, and hold your paintbox in your left hand; or you can rest your paintbox on some firm footing within easy reach beside you and hold your block of paper on your lap with your left hand.

I usually follow the latter procedure while painting the sky, particularly if I am painting an active, cloudy sky and am floating in colors very wet and want them to flow as I tilt the paper one way or another. Then I complete the rest of the picture with the block placed on an easel, on a campstool, on a box, or on the ground and hold paint pan in hand.

Most watercolorists paint skies first and then let them dry before tackling the rest of the picture. The time depends on temperature and humidity, but it is just a matter of minutes.

The easiest and, I think, the best way to paint a sky is to mix a rather rich wash of the color or colors you want in your mixing pan. Remember that skies are not always blue, nor are they all blue even on a reasonably clear day. Then rinse out your brush and apply clear water over the entire sky, except for areas you have indicated for clouds, until you can see a thin layer of water flow one direction or another as you tilt your block. Then start flowing in your color rapidly, beginning at the top.

If you study a clear blue sky, you will notice that

it is usually a deep blue overhead but fades into a gray-blue as it nears the horizon.

Begin with a wash of Cobalt Blue at the top of your paper. Sweep your brush quickly across your paper, each time just overlapping your last brush stroke. Begin to introduce Cerulean Blue as you go down your sky, diminishing the Cobalt in your mix until you are using a pure Cerulean wash. As you near your horizon, increase the water in your brush in relation to pigment and begin to add just a touch of Alizarin Crimson to achieve a gray-blue. When you reach the horizon in your sketch, or the point at which objects in your picture meet the sky, flick or squeeze the moisture from your brush and pick up the excess moisture along the lower margin of your sky.

When painting a cloudy sky, do not wash color evenly from top to bottom but, starting at the top, flow color in at different places and angles. Depending on the effect you seek to produce, use deep

Stand up and step back once in a while to see how your picture is coming. Do this when you have finished your sky area and are waiting for it to dry. It is a fine opportunity to plan the rest of your attack, the order in which you will paint different areas, the intensity of the color you will use. But stand back at other times, too, to see your picture as a whole and to appraise the effect you are achieving.

First Step. *Draw a pencil outline sketch of subject. The example here was sketched more heavily than would normally be necessary, in order to make sure that it would photograph and reproduce successfully.*

Second Step. *Brush clear water over sky and cloudy areas which are to be covered with color. Follow quickly with color while area is still moist. White edges of clouds are left untouched with color but softened here and there by picking up surrounding color with Kleenex or a clean brush. Wait for sky to dry before painting contiguous areas.*

Third Step. *Either water or land areas could have been painted next. In this case, water area was painted first and then land down to, but not including, the foreground. Because some contrast of color seemed desirable in the grass in the immediate foreground, it was left until last.*

Fourth Step. *Now for the dark areas. It is usually best to paint dark areas last because dark colors can be painted over light in watercolors but not the reverse. In this picture the trees were painted, then the ramshackle old structure at the left.*

grays, blue-grays, brown-grays, and blacks, at the same time tilting the watercolor block from side to side and up and down so that your colors flow into the approximation of cloud formations before they dry. Lighter contrasts and billowy effects can be achieved by picking up some of the color in strategic spots with a wadded piece of Kleenex.

"At this point," one of our best professional watercolorists once told me, "I get up and stretch, light a cigarette, and rest for a moment while my sky dries and while I stand back and take a look at my sketch. At the same time, I reexamine my subject, fixing in my mind the relative values I want to give various components of my picture." As a matter of fact, you will find it desirable to stand back from your work every once in a while to see how your picture as a whole is coming. It pays off in end results and in personal comfort, for one gets cramped and stiff from sitting too long in one position.

In completing the rest of your picture after your sky is painted, you can choose between two procedures. You can paint light areas first and then follow with dark, or you can reverse the procedure and follow dark with light. For an amateur, I believe, the first procedure is best. It is a little easier to tell how deep your shadows and dark areas must be for sharp contrast after the light areas are painted, and it is also possible to darken light areas by painting over them with darker shades if you find they have dried out lighter than you intended. Furthermore, if you do your dark areas last, you will find you are carrying in your brush the darker colors with which you can put in shadows and accents essential in your light areas.

Incidentally, in making your original outline sketch it is desirable to indicate where the shadows fall. The sun will be moving all the time you are at work on your watercolor, and as a result the position of shadows will change. In your finished watercolor you must be consistent. The position of all your shadows must reveal sunlight from the same direction. Hence the desirability of "freezing" them in your pencil outline sketch.

Never use black in painting shadows. Areas in shadow are actually in most cases luminous with color. Transparent but darker colors should be used. The shady side of a red barn is merely a

Fifth Step. *Complete the foreground, then add the accents and shadows which lend form and interest to the picture. Both brush strokes and lines scratched with the point of a pocketknife help to give the impression of ragged grass in the foreground. At this point, erase pencil marks if they were sketched in too heavily—as they were in this picture. Finally, place the picture in a mat. The colors gain new strength and the whole picture is stepped up by the contrast with the white mat. Another "lift" is achieved when picture and mat are framed under glass.*

darker red. Grass in sunshine is usually a yellow-green; in shadow it is a dark green or blue-green. The shaded side of a tree trunk is a darker gray or darker brown than the side which is in sunlight. The shaded side of a white house is usually a blue-gray, with other colors reflected from adjacent trees or shrubs. Shadows thrown on areas in sunshine are surpainted over the light areas after the latter have been painted and have had time to dry.

If you are like most amateurs, you will find that in your earlier attempts you will have to fight a tendency to approach watercolors timidly, to make small pictures, to use weak colors and tiny brush strokes, and to put in minute details with great fidelity to the subject before you. Fight these tendencies like the plague.

Watercolors should be tackled boldly, in fact almost recklessly. Resist the temptation to use a small watercolor block. Start with a sheet not less than 12 by 18 inches and preferably 16 by 20 inches. Make a drawing that fills the paper with your subject. Use rich, strong washes and color. Make vivid contrasts by using deep, dark color in your shadows. Work with the largest brush you can in every area of your picture, reserving your smaller brushes for subject matter—details of windows and doorways, of masts or twigs and branches of trees—which involves unavoidable detail. Use bold brush strokes. Crowd yourself to work rapidly. Flat surfaces, such as the roofs of buildings, you should flow in swiftly with generous brush strokes, mixing your colors in part on the paper as you go. Side walls, except for window and doorway openings, should also be handled with good-size brushes and full strokes rather than niggling, timid little dabs. Even the shadows under the eaves of house roofs are more interesting if handled casually and without too much precision.

Don't be afraid of making errors. Of course, we amateurs are going to make mistakes, but even if we do, it's wise to go ahead and finish the picture. Sometimes accidents or mistakes are lost in the finished watercolor; sometimes, as I have pointed out, they turn out to be fortunate and actually enhance the end result. And anyway we learn from our own mistakes; we learn by doing.

It would be amazing indeed if all our attempts brought successful results. There is no reason to feel frustrated or to give up this hobby just because our first few pictures turn out to be disappointing. As a matter of fact, the best of professional artists will frankly admit that only a minority of their pictures turn out well enough to justify offering for public sale. It has been my experience that less than half of my pictures are even worth placing in mats, let alone in frames. Of course as your skills improve with experience and practice, you achieve a higher percentage of acceptable results; but, as in golf or tennis, it is only rarely that you are at the top of your form.

Above everything else, don't be distressed or discouraged by your first few pictures. I'm reminded of a friend who said to me one day, "I tried watercolor painting recently. I got out in the back yard and tried to paint our garden as seen from our terrace." He shook his head sadly. "The result was terrible. I've given up painting. I guess I'm no artist."

To which I replied, "Tell me, Tom—how good was your first game of golf?" A slowly comprehending grin spread over his face.

chapter 6 LESSONS FROM EXPERIENCE

One bright summer morning, while I was in the midst of a watercolor, two men walked up behind me. Without a word of greeting or comment they stood silently for five or ten minutes watching my progress. I had chosen a spot on a back street in an old whaling village on Long Island not far from where I have spent my summer holidays for a good many years. The scene included an old one-car garage at one side, a rather scrubby, ill-kept back yard, and, through it, the rear exposures of some two- and three-story buildings which faced away from me on the main street. The roofs of the buildings were uneven and colorful. Their walls looked a little unsteady, and their upper floors, apparently occupied as living quarters, were decorated by casually placed stairways and porches.

As my two observers walked away, one of them, evidently thinking he was out of earshot, snorted, "Don't artists pick the damnedest things to paint!"

A half-hour later a young woman approached rather timidly and asked, "Do you mind if I look at your picture?"

"Not at all," I replied, "as long as you realize I'm just an amateur indulging in my favorite hobby."

When she saw what I was doing, she exclaimed with enthusiasm and went on to say, "You know, I've always loved that view from here. My husband and I live on the second floor of that middle building with the covered porch out back. From it we get a lovely view of the harbor. We run the local weekly newspaper. The office and printing shop are on the ground floor."

Finally, after a long pause, came the cautious question: "What do you do with your pictures after they are finished?"

I explained that I usually matted them and saved them, sometimes had them framed and hung at home or in our summer cottage, and once in a great while gave them to friends who expressed a desire to have them.

"If you should decide you don't want this one, would you let my husband and me buy it?" she asked tactfully. "We probably couldn't pay what it's really worth but we'd love to have it."

I am almost ashamed to admit that after so high

a compliment—a sincere offer to buy—I did not give the picture to her; but it turned out quite well as my things go, and it has now hung for several years in the living room of our summer cottage. There it receives almost universally favorable comment from warm-hearted and uncritical friends.

Why do artists pick the subjects they do? Why do they usually select old and ramshackle structures to paint instead of well-kept houses and modern buildings? The answer is simple. Such subjects make better pictures. On various occasions I have done watercolors of the winter or summer homes of my friends, but even those that have turned out fairly well have a tendency to look like architectural perspective renderings. The well-kept perfection of the subjects makes the finished watercolors look too stiff, too lacking in the variety of color and interest that are inherent in the things which artists —amateurs and professionals alike—find most appealing. Roofs which sag a little, structural lines which lean a little off the perpendicular, walls which have acquired the patina which only time and the elements can produce—these are the things to look for in selecting a watercolor subject. And if you exaggerate all of them a little in your picture, you are well within the limits of artistic license.

One afternoon recently I did a watercolor of an old, deserted Victorian house on the outskirts of a neighboring village on Long Island. It had an ornate mansard roof and decrepit porches halfway round the house; the walls which couldn't have been painted in the last twenty years had weathered into nice warm shades of grays and browns. Some of the windows were shuttered or boarded up, while others were half shaded by faded blue blinds. The lawn, or what had once been a lawn, had grown waist-high with ragged grass and weeds, turned yellow and brown in the sun. The house and foreground stood out against a background of dark-green trees. It made a lovely watercolor, and I felt a warm glow of satisfaction when I matted it at home and added a few finishing touches.

That evening we had cocktails with friends who had spent several summers in the neighboring community where I had done my watercolor that afternoon. Our hostess asked whether I had done any painting recently. I told her with enthusiasm about the old house I had painted. As I described it, a look of incredulity came over her face and she exclaimed, "But why in the world would you choose that subject? Everyone over in B—— considers that place a terrible eyesore."

Since then I have shown the picture to several friends whose artistic judgment I hold in high regard. They like it, and some of them even think it is one of the best watercolors I have ever done.

The moral is this: pick your own subjects. Don't let friends or family pick them for you. Choose those you can tackle with enthusiasm, but in the process don't confine your selection to things which have a picture-postcard quality of perfection. They will rarely turn out to be good watercolor subjects.

By the same token, once you have chosen a subject, don't feel that you must reproduce it exactly as you find it. Don't have so much respect for nature that you won't move a tree, or draw together a scattered group of buildings now and then if it makes a better picture, or put in a winding roadway if it helps to give a path for the eye to follow. By all means give sufficient emphasis to what you want to present as the focal point of interest in your watercolor so that there is no doubt as to your intent.

I have a daughter—now married—who was just entering her teens when I began to paint watercolors. For many years she was my severest but most constructive critic. Again and again I have come home after a half day of sketching, matted up a watercolor, set it up for her to see, and asked her opinion. Her favorite query if I failed to establish clearly a focal point of interest has always been "What's it a picture of?"

When you are uncomfortably aware that, for some reason, your picture hasn't quite come off, that's a pretty devastating question. But it is a question I find well worth asking myself after I have chosen my subject and am about to start my outline sketch. "What is this going to be a picture of?"

Let's assume for a moment that we have chosen a typical barnyard scene. It probably includes a big old weather-beaten barn, a silo, maybe a corncrib, one or two other buildings scattered about, and some cattle at the watering trough. What are we going to make a picture of? Should we make this a picture of that wonderful old barn with a silo attached, or should we make it a picture of the towering old silo which happens to be attached to a barn? Or should we make it a picture of cattle at the watering trough, with a background of barn and silo?

We may use all the elements I have mentioned in whichever picture we choose to paint, but we will give them different values, depending on what we have decided to paint a picture of. When we have settled that question, we use every device at our command to subtly give the element we have chosen the greatest value in our picture; to make it, in other words, the focal point of attention.

We can achieve that end by a variety of means. It can be accomplished in part by the position from which we view the subject and the size to which we play it up in our sketch. Things can be subdued by being thrown in shadow. They will attract your eye if they are painted in vivid sunshine against a deeply shadowed background. Your eye can be carried to them by such devices as a path or a roadway or the direction in which a shadow falls. These things must be done subtly to be done well, but they are all part of a painter's stock in trade.

Handling the elements of our subject in ways which make our finished picture hang together in comfortable balance and with a focal point of attention to which the eye naturally gravitates is all part of that mystifying achievement known as good composition. It is accomplished by the techniques I have already described, but it is also affected by our choice of harmonious colors and particularly by the repetition of the same color in different parts of our picture.

For example, if we decide to paint our silo a faded red in our barnyard scene, we should pick up that same color somewhere else in our picture. Or if our barn is a weather-beaten natural-wood color, we should seek an opportunity to repeat it in other buildings or in fences. This repetition of color gives a "tone" to a watercolor. It also helps to subdue elements which would otherwise stand out alone, competing with each other for attention, instead of merging into a harmonious whole.

One of the things we amateurs have to learn is to simplify our subjects to the point where they are manageable. Literal-minded persons like myself have an inclination to draw and paint with great precision. We paint what we see, and until we break ourselves of the habit, we add to our difficulties by becoming slaves to every detail in the scene before us. We paint leaves, twigs, and branches, rather than trees. We paint individual trees when we should be painting woods. We paint windows, doors, shingles, and clapboards when we should be painting houses.

What we really should strive for is to transmit to others through the medium of our picture the impression our subject has made upon us. We want to put on paper our interpretation of what we see, and we actually see only a limited amount of detail. Our problem, therefore, is to simplify our subourselves of the habit, we add to our difficulties by the medium of watercolor.

Suppose for a moment that we are doing a watercolor of an old house, one of those lovely old gray-shingle and white-trim places which you see so often in New England villages, particularly along the coast. We'll determine the general tone of one wall and then wash it in, allowing for some variation of color as we go along in order to give that characteristic weather-beaten look. We won't try to paint each shingle by itself or even each row of shingles. Later when we are putting in shadows and accents we can come back to this area and paint a few shadow lines to suggest rows of shingles. And we may even decide, if the house is very close to us, to indicate just a suggestion of individual shingles at the nearest point but fading them out as they go away from us.

Mountains have always caused me trouble. I really never began to paint them with even the most modest success until I began to realize that they must be greatly simplified. We simply cannot put in every crevice, ravine, cliff, rock, and tree. All we can do is strive for the effect of what we see.

The same principles of simplification apply to the painting of buildings with many windows. Take a tall office building for example. A watercolor is much more effective if it includes only a few windows—just enough to suggest that there are hundreds of them—

One can suggest things in a picture but leave much to the imagination. Take the tall building in the background in this quick watercolor sketch, for example. The windows are merely suggested, not painted individually down the whole side of the building, and yet the effect of hundreds of windows is there. Incidentally, note that the building was painted in before the blue sky area had dried. As a result the wash laid on the building began to creep into the sky on the upper right hand side of the building. Still another example of creep is visible at the lower right in the foreground. Here I allowed a ripple of color to rest too long before picking it up with a relatively moisture-free brush. As a result water from the ripple began to creep back into the color of the building.

than if the artist tries to draw in each one of them.

In the foreground of our pictures we should put in more detail. There we can even paint quite precisely a few dangling leaves, or the gnarled trunk of a tree, or a few blades of grass. But in middle distance and background, suggesting what we see is much better than inserting every detail.

Simplify, suggest, but leave something to the imagination. These are commands we should repeat to ourselves again and again until we can resist the temptation to put in everything we see and until we can restrain ourselves from sketching everything meticulously.

One of the surest ways to accomplish our ends is to use the largest brush we can possibly paint with in a given area of our picture. Some details can be put in only with a fine-pointed brush, but you will be surprised how effectively a large brush can be used and how much easier it is to avoid being overly precise.

The accents—light, shadow, and depth of color —which lend character, dimension, and life to a watercolor are applied in part as one is in the process of painting. But I find it advisable after I get home to mount my watercolor in a white mat and take another look at it. It is difficult to appraise your result accurately until you have done so. A white mat gives a watercolor a lift that is startling. The contrast of plain white mat with color makes the color seem richer and more vivid.

Once your picture is matted, set it up on a table or chair, stand back from it 8 or 10 feet, and take a good look at it. You will find in all probability that a shadow is a little weak here, a color a little insipid there. You will want to accent some of these things a little more for better effects.

Remember you can intensify color values by covering weak color with strong. You can cover a light shade with dark, but you cannot cover dark with light and have a happy result. As a matter of fact, you should keep all your surpainting to a minimum, for you to run the risk of muddying your watercolor down to dirty tones of gray. A certain amount of surpainting is inevitable for an amateur, and very few professionals can manage a watercolor without it. When you do surpaint, leave little breaks in which the old color shows through. It avoids the danger of making the surpainted area too dead and heavy-looking in relation to the rest of the picture.

But don't overdo this business of accenting. If you insist on being a perfectionist, you can keep on touching up a picture forever. Unless you are willing to settle for a little less than what you consider ideal, you will find you have gone too far and spoiled your picture.

When you are all through, keep your picture in a mat as long as you are likely to show it to anyone. Never show an unmatted picture. You will not do the picture or yourself justice.

chapter 7 SOLUTION OF COMMON PROBLEMS

Because the sky areas are important in most pictures and are part of almost every picture, I will repeat and elaborate here on some of the points I made in an earlier chapter (Chapter 5, Your First Watercolor).

There was a time when skies bothered me very much indeed. I could never seem to get a good smooth wash in a blue sky. It always came out streaked with brush strokes. And as for the white clouds which I occasionally tried to reproduce, their edges came out hard and the clouds looked as if they were pasted on my paper against a blue background.

The secret, I finally learned, is to wet the portion of your paper which is devoted to sky area. The wetting can be done with a sponge or with a watercolor brush dipped again and again in clear water. Put enough water on the paper so that you can see it flow from side to side as you tilt your watercolor block one way or the other, but not enough so that it will run down over the rest of the paper which you have reserved for other subject matter.

If you want to leave pure white clouds, don't cover them with water; but when you flow in color, don't bring it right up to the edge of the dry cloud area except in places where you intentionally want to give your cloud a clearly defined edge. If you look at clouds in the sky, you will note that some edges are sharply defined, while others are soft and fleecy.

With the sky area thoroughly moist, you are ready to flow in your color. Using horizontal brush strokes, lay it in strong, with plenty of pigment at the top of the paper; let each new brush stroke overlap the last; vary your shade of blue slightly, even putting in an occasional light touch of green. As you approach the horizon, add more and more water and finally shade your sky into gray-blue or lavender.

Skies will repay lots of thoughtful study and practice. They have much to do with the mood of your picture. They can carry the cheerful mood of a bright, clear day, or the threatening atmosphere of an approaching storm. They can be active or inert. They can play a conspicuous part in your picture, or they can provide a subdued background to the things you are emphasizing.

One thing you will quickly discover, if you adopt the method of wetting your sky area before you

Beach at Antigua

The active sky, the pounding surf, the wind-swept palms and ground cover in this watercolor all contribute to the feeling of wind and movement. The composition, with large palm at the left and two smaller palms to the right, is well balanced and the beach and shore line provide a sweeping but not too obvious path for the eye to follow into the distance.

start to paint, is that you will have to saturate your brush more heavily with pigment than you do when working on a dry surface. The water already on your paper will reduce the intensity of your color. You will find, too, that you can do much of your mixing of paint right on the wet surface of your paper rather than in your mixing pan.

During the painting of the sky, keep a wadded piece of Kleenex handy to soften the edges of your clouds or to pick up excess water or color if it becomes unmanageable.

In general, the same procedures work well in painting gray skies. Remember in painting them, as well as in painting blue skies, that no sky is ever one unvarying shade of color. In any overcast sky there are warm brownish grays and blacks as well as colder bluish grays. In your experiments with overcast skies, flow colors in boldly, even recklessly, and let them flow around over your sky area. Tilt your paper occasionally, and let your colors run back and forth or up and down. You will be pleasantly surprised to find how well this casual treatment turns out.

No matter what you think of your sky when it is finished, do not let it keep you from going ahead with the rest of your picture. Many a time I have been unhappy about a sky but have found that when the picture was finished, it didn't look badly at all.

We amateurs can learn a great deal about handling skies if we are careful observers of the work of good professional artists. This is one of many ways in which visits to the art galleries and to the watercolor shows pay off. It is equally helpful to study the reproductions of the work of distinguished watercolorists in such magazines as *The American Artist.*

It is interesting to note how rarely our best artists paint blue skies. The great temptation of amateurs is to paint nothing else. And note, too, how boldly our top-flight watercolorists use color in either bright or forbidding skies, how much of the mood of their pictures depends on their treatment of skies.

You can handle water in much the same way that you handle a sky, except that you cannot let color flow back into previously painted areas. Water must be handled with horizontal brush strokes, as you carry your wash down the paper, in order to give the effect of a smooth surface. I wouldn't attempt to paint a stormy sea or a rough surf until I had had lots of experience with watercolors.

If you study a body of water carefully, you will observe that it mirrors the color of the sky but that it is not the same color from horizon to foreground. Sometimes it is darker at the horizon and lighter as it comes near you. At other times, depending on the position of the sun, it is a deeper, stronger color in the foreground and grows lighter as it approaches the horizon. You can take an artist's liberties and paint it the way that suits your convenience and fits your picture better.

In your study of water you will discover another thing, namely, that it is not always blue. As a matter of fact, it is rarely a clear, deep blue. Its color varies into shades of gray or green, depending on the amount of light playing on it, how deep or how shallow it is, whether clouds have cast a shadow over part of its surface, and how white the sand is in shallow areas.

After the basic coloring of your water has dried on your paper, you can look for ripples or reflections—reflections of docks, boats, and buildings. They can be painted in over the water in your picture. In doing so, you will find that water is almost always in movement, no matter how calm it may seem at first glance. As a result, reflections will usually follow wavering and broken lines.

Boats and boatyards, docks and waterfronts are a source of unending interest to most artists and a prolific source of subject matter. The problem for the amateur is to sort out the things which make a good picture and to avoid getting tangled up in too much detail. "What is it going to be a picture of?" is a particularly important question to ask when one takes an exploratory stroll around a boatyard, looking for a subject that sparks imagination and arouses enthusiasm. And "Keep it simple" is also a wise admonition at this point.

As a matter of fact, it is pretty difficult to keep it simple, for most of us who have not grown up at the water's edge and therefore are not familiar with boats begin to discover what a wide variety of boats there are and how many differences appear in the shape of their hulls, their general lines, their deckhouses, their masts, and their rigging. A boatyard scene usually involves a more carefully drawn outline sketch than almost any other type of watercolor.

The masts and halyards of sailboats against the background of sky, buildings, other boats, or foliage present a minor but easily solved problem. The top of a mast may be dark against the sky, but it may also be light against background material. A painter treats it accordingly, painting the top of the mast with a small pointed brush full of pigment, but washing it out to lighter shades as he paints down through the background. If he is afraid he will cover over the mast area while he is painting his background, he can use a masking fluid to cover it, erasing the dried fluid with artgum eraser after the background has dried. Halyards can be painted dark against a light sky, but they are such delicate lines that the only way to make them show against a dark background is to scratch them out with the point of a knife after the background has been painted. In this way the white paper will show through, restoring the effect of the rigging. Don't try to make these lines continuous and of equal value for their entire length. Let them come and go, fading out and returning; otherwise they will play too conspicuous a part in the picture.

Incidentally, a sharp-pointed knife can be used in dark areas to suggest blades of grass or twigs of trees or can be applied to a painted area where a highlight is desirable.

Mountains, as I have pointed out elsewhere, present peculiar problems. Their treatment, in the main, calls for a simplification of what one sees. Sometimes they must be shifted with relation to foreground material, or vice versa, to achieve good composition. Certainly we don't want the peak of a conspicuous mountain smack in the middle of our picture.

We must make up our minds right at the start that we cannot put in every detail we see on a mountainside. We must select the salient characteristics of the scene and of our subject and arrange them for good composition, submerging the values of some and emphasizing those of others. The farther away our mountain is, the less detail we should include, until a mountain in the distance becomes just a hazy blue shadow against the sky. In the middle distance shadows and minor variations of color can suggest the rugged outlines of a mountain, while in the foreground we can begin to give real definition to individual rocks and trees.

I have tried painting mountains in the Rockies of Montana, in the Palm Springs area of Southern California, and in the Virgin Islands, with varying degrees of success. Mountains differ in each area in color and conformation. That fact alone adds to the interesting challenge they offer. The one common denominator I have found in tackling all of them is—I repeat—that they must be simplified, that one can only give an impression of them, that too much detail in any other than foreground subject matter leads to an unhappy result.

An amateur watercolorist does not need to be also a naturalist to discover that there are many different types of trees. He cannot help but be impressed with that fact as soon as he undertakes his first picture. The structure of their trunks and branches differs and their foliage varies in density of growth, in color, and in conformation. Only when a tree is placed in the immediate foreground does one make any attempt to delineate even a few individual leaves, in order to suggest the character of the mass as a whole. But it does add interest to a picture to differentiate the trees to some degree.

It is worthwhile, therefore, to pay considerable attention, particularly in foreground and middle-distance elements, to the general form and color of the trees. Do their branches reach for the sky, do they arch gracefully, do they reach straight out horizontally, or do they droop toward the ground? Do they have smooth, round, perpendicular trunks, or are they gnarled and tortuous? Is their foliage sparse, or bunched so that patches of sky and glimpses of branches show through? And are their branches and trunks white or gray, brown or black, or a mixture of colors, in the light in which you are painting them? These are all questions which must be answered in part in your outline sketch and more fully with brush and pigment as you paint your watercolor.

In painting trees, paint the leaves first if a branch is very close at hand and then the foliage masses, being careful not to paint them in so solidly that you leave no openings through which to show glimpses of the trunks and branches. Watch for the variety of colors that are to be found in foliage masses, the lighter greens on the side from which your light is coming, the darker greens in shadow, and the different shades of greens and browns to be found if one looks for them. They add richness and effect to the wooded areas of your picture.

Make the most of the shapes of tree trunks and branches which are usually painted in after the foliage dries. Careful use of color and of light and shade on tree trunks will give them their cylindrical effect. Each type of tree has its own characteristics, which can be reproduced with reasonable fidelity provided one is observant.

The greatest help I have ever derived from any source on the handling of trees has come from the late Ted Kautzky's wonderful and beautifully illustrated book *Painting Trees and Landscapes in Watercolor* (Reinhold Publishing Corporation, 1952). A master of watercolor painting himself, Kautzky has presented his subject with a directness and simplicity—and an abundance of skillful illustration—that is tremendously helpful to beginner and advanced amateur alike. A copy of Mr. Kautzky's book is one of my highly prized possessions.

When we come to painting in areas such as lawns, fields of grain, and pastures, it pays to stop a moment and study the varying shades of green and tan we have before us, depending on the season, the sunlight, and the nature of the terrain. Fields in the distance take on rather even color characteristics, but in the foreground we will usually discover a wide variety of shades.

Remember that paint flows quite smoothly from brush to paper when the brush is held almost vertical. When the brush is laid almost flat and stroked quickly across rough paper, it leaves the indentations free of pigment. We can use the latter technique to fine effect in areas where we want to suggest brilliant sunshine on grass or ground. Brush strokes should follow the contour of the land. The impression of grass or grain can then be enhanced with a few delicate vertical brush strokes in foreground and carefully chosen middle-distance areas after our first coat has dried.

Rocks, rock walls, or a rocky shore line look difficult at first, but they really are not too big an undertaking for an amateur. Light and shadow play on their irregular surfaces. Some of these pick up the color of the sky, blending into darker shades as their rounded or irregular surfaces curve downward into shadows, where they are not directly reached by the sun. There are deep, sharp, dark shadows in the crevices between rocks, while shadows of medium intensity are thrown upon one rock by another. Careful treatment of these shadows lends form to the stones, while the uneven application of the basic color of the rocks delineates their true appearance. You can simplify rocky groups to advantage at times by making individual rocks bigger than they really are, thus leaving yourself with fewer of them to paint.

One of the problems we amateurs face quite early in our painting experience lies in making our houses and barns, for example, look as if they rested comfortably in the ground instead of being perched precariously upon it. We want them to look as if they belonged there—as if they had been there for years. The same is true of trunks of trees. The effect can be obtained by softening the edge of a structure or tree trunk where it meets the ground. Add to the wall or tree trunk at the point of contact a touch of the color which you will subsequently use as you complete that part of the picture. It can also be enhanced by avoiding a smooth, hard line where ground and building or tree trunk meet. Watch for shrubbery or undergrowth or ragged tufts of grass which you can allow to run up into the more solid areas of walls and tree trunks.

Something of the same problem arises in trying to make boats ride comfortably in water rather than sit uneasily on top of it. Softening the line of the hull where it meets the water and adding a reflection in the water helps to accomplish this end.

Unless we simply cannot resist the temptation to include them, it's a pretty good idea for us amateurs to leave human figures out of our earlier watercolors. Once we have begun to master the use of our materials, we can experiment with figures.

When you have reached this stage, I suggest that you start first with some experimental sketches. Try drawing a few sketches of men and women. Keep them simple, because in watercolor painting we will rarely want to have people in the immediate foreground of our pictures. Make them only 2 or 3 inches tall on your sketch pad.

We are going to try first to draw human figures in reasonably sound proportions. That is, we want their heads the right size for their bodies, their shoulders approximately the right width, and their arms and legs the right length.

Frank A. Staples in his book *Watercolor Painting Is Fun* (McGraw-Hill Book Company, Inc., 1948) comes up with the interesting observation that a man is usually seven heads high, a woman six and one-half heads, and a young child three and a half. I have found that observation extremely helpful. If you decide on the size a man's head should be in your picture, you can multiply it by 7 and have the over-all height of the man. Or if you decide on the height you want your man to be, you allocate one-seventh of that height to his head.

Once we have succeeded in getting a few figures sketched in reasonable human proportions, we must begin to think of how to paint them. What is the color of their clothing? How do shadows fall in the folds of their garments? We want the greatest simplicity we can achieve and still give the effect of living people who look normal in the environment in which we place them. Here again, practice will help.

If you lack human models, it's a good idea to save a few clippings of pictures from the picture magazines: street scenes and landscapes in which human figures appear in some relationship to each other and to familiar structures. And it is particularly important to observe how figures are handled by professional watercolorists in their pictures.

Remember that our brief study of perspective in drawing brought out the fact that things seem to grow smaller, the farther they are away from us; that lines drawn along the tops and bottoms of telegraph poles seem to converge as they approach the horizon or vanishing point. The same is true of human figures in our pictures. Men in the background appear smaller than men in the foreground, even though they are actually of the same height. They must be drawn accordingly in relation to each other and also in relation to such things as the doors and windows in houses, barns, and buildings in our landscapes.

Human figures in a watercolor picture have a strong tendency to attract the eye, particularly if they are figures of people in action. We must keep them somewhat subdued, therefore, both in color and in clarity of detail, unless we want them to be the focal point of attention. They frequently add interest to a picture, provided they have a natural part to play in it; but they can spoil a picture if we let them run away with the spotlight, so to speak, when we intended them to play only a minor part in the composition.

Animals and birds, particularly birds soaring in flight, offer many of the same opportunities and the same problems as human figures in landscape painting. They are worth experimenting with as one progresses.

Portrait painting in watercolors? Let's drop that subject like a hot potato. It requires a proficiency in the handling of watercolors which few amateurs ever attain, plus that rare talent, the ability to get a likeness. Few portrait painters attempt the use of watercolors. Their customary medium is oils.

In reviewing some of the problems all beginners face in watercolor painting, I hope I have not made them appear so formidable as to be discouraging. Certainly that has not been my intent. I come back to a statement I made in an earlier chapter. If there were no problems in watercolor painting, it would not be the challenging and fascinating hobby that it is. To repeat my earlier simile, it would be like playing golf on a course that was flat, all fairways, and free of traps or bunkers.

As a matter of fact, each picture one undertakes involves new problems which test one's skill—and at times one's patience—but which add unending variety and interest to watercolor painting.

chapter 8 ADVENTURES WITH WATERCOLORS

One of the reasons more people do not take up watercolor painting as a hobby is the feeling that one must travel to some distant, picturesque, and unusual spot to find good subjects. That can be disproved by a visit to almost any comprehensive watercolor show. The range of subject matter is amazing. I believe it can truthfully be said that things which make good pictures depend more on the perception and imagination of the artist—what he sees in a subject—than on the subject itself. It should be added, of course, that the success of a picture depends also on the skills of the artist, but the subject matter is there for any discerning person to work with.

I do not mean to minimize the stimulus of new scenes and new places, particularly if they provide a different and more colorful type of landscape from that to which we are accustomed. Change is as stimulating to an artist as it is to any other tourist—and perhaps even more so. But watercolor painting provides an amateur artist with opportunities for relaxation and "escape" within his normal environment. As a matter of fact, he will find that the easiest subjects to paint are those with which he is most familiar. New scenes and new places are stimulating but they also bring new problems in painting. Your own home town or the country around it is as good a place as any to start painting.

New York, where I make my home, offers limitless possibilities for street scenes of every description, waterfront and dockyard pictures, and landscapes in the city's parks. Every city has something to offer. Of course, if you decide to paint in a city, you have to be prepared to have an audience. An amateur needs courage to plant a campstool on a city sidewalk, on a waterfront street, or in a park. I'll have to confess there are spots in New York City where I know good watercolor subjects are waiting to be painted, but where so many people pass constantly that I have never nerved myself to do a sketch. In a few cases I have solved the problem by sitting in my car and making a pencil sketch with color notes—pencil notations as to the color in different areas of the sketch—and in a few instances I have even done watercolors while sitting in the car. That, however, is pretty difficult, for it means working in cramped quarters and in constant fear of spilling water or paint in my lap or on the seat of the car.

But I have learned to screw up my courage to the point of picking a spot in public now and then, usually where there isn't a constant procession of people passing, and brazening it out beneath the gaze of passers-by who stop to look over my shoulder. For the most part they are very considerate, and when they are not, it is because they unintentionally get too close or manage to get in the way. And I find that most persons, although driven by irresistible curiosity, seem almost as timid about looking at one's work as we amateurs are about having them do so. Some come and go without a word; others exchange friendly greetings and make an occasional comment, always kindly, and only in the rarest instances critical, about one's progress with his picture. I usually feel constrained to explain that I am an amateur just painting for fun, but if I'm deeply absorbed, I don't even bother to do that.

Once I become engrossed in what I'm doing, I lose the self-consciousness with which I start a sketch in a place where people are almost certain to pass. After that I find it doesn't bother me to have visitors. In fact, I can carry on a conversation with them without interrupting my work. These conversations are one of the minor adventures of watercolor painting. They give one an insight into the lives of the people in the area which no casual visitor would ever get. To anyone who is at all gregarious they are heart-warming experiences.

One warm spring Saturday morning a year or so ago, I tossed my painting equipment and a camp-stool in the back seat of the car and set out for Brooklyn by way of the Battery tunnel. I had explored the waterfront down toward the Narrows some time before and had come to the conclusion that the shipyards and docks in that section hold a wealth of paintable subjects. After a little further scouting when I reached the waterfront, I found myself on a street at the water's edge from which long, covered docks jutted out into a spacious salt-water inlet. Tied up at one of these docks was a colorful freighter riding high out of water with a wide expanse of rusty, red hull showing below what would normally be her water line.

But there were problems. The ship was tied up about halfway out toward the end of the long dock. If I painted her from the street, I would have to do her almost head on. I preferred to do the ship at an angle, but to do that I would have to go out on the next dock to the south. That obviously wasn't going to be easy, as there was a guard at the entrance.

I parked the car and surveyed the scene again on foot. There was nothing for it but to try to get out on the dock. I walked over to the guard and asked, "Will it be all right if I go out on the dock?"

"Nope," was his laconic reply.

"All I want to do," I said, "is to paint a picture of the freighter tied up at the next dock."

"Can't let you out. You'll have to ask the boss."

"Who is he?"

"He's the super."

"Where is he?"

"Out on the dock."

I waited. Far out in what, by contrast with the bright sunshine outside, were the shadowy recesses of the covered dock I could see men working. Finally one man separated himself from the group and strolled leisurely toward the entrance where I was waiting. I walked out a few paces to meet him and made my wants known. He looked me over from head to foot before replying, then said, "I guess it will be all right, but don't fall overboard."

I laughed. "That," I said, "is the last thing I want to do."

Carrying my campstool, watercolor block, and sketch pad, and my bag of watercolor essentials, I walked out on the dock a hundred feet or more and found a small door through one of the huge sliding sections which walled the side of the big steel shed covering the dock. Stepping through it, I found myself on a 5-foot walk 10 or 12 feet above the water. It was shaded from the sun and in an ideal position from which to do the picture of the freighter I had in mind.

Unfolding my campstool, I sat down, took a final look at the scene through my finder to determine how broad a field I wanted to include, and then went to work on my preliminary outline sketch. I had just finished it and was squeezing pigment from paint tubes into my paintbox when I became aware that someone had walked up behind me. I looked back over my shoulder to find the super examining my sketch closely.

"Nice," he remarked; "you really got it."

"Thanks. I'm glad you like it," I said as I went ahead with my preparations. Just then I squeezed the last bit of pigment from one of my tubes and tossed it overboard.

"Hey," said the super, "careful, or you'll disturb old Davy Jordan."

"Don't you mean Davy Jones?" I asked.

"No, Davy Jordan. He's an old fellow who worked on the docks here for thirty years. Slipped and fell overboard two days ago when we were unloading a lighter. Haven't seen hide nor hair of him since." He paused a moment, leaned over the side and looked down at the murky, uninviting water. "The police boat dragged around here for him on both sides of the dock for the last two days. Gave up yesterday. Said he must be tangled up in something down there or the tide has carried him away by this time."

I hitched my campstool a little farther away from the dock's edge and went on about my work. The super came and went all morning long, obviously very much interested by this time in my progress. Occasionally he pointed out a detail I had missed, determined that I make a photographic likeness of the ship. He was a firm but kindly and admiring mentor.

A tugboat came churning in to lash on to a barge tied up at the dock and pull her out of the slip. There was an exchange of robust greetings with the super and an inquiry about Davy Jordan. Then she was on her way again.

"I used to ship on a tug myself," remarked the super, who was still standing behind me. "Not a bad life. Good pay and good food, but long hours."

"Is that so? Why did you come ashore?"

"Well," he said, "it ain't no life for a family man. Five days on board each shift, twenty-four hours a day, and then a couple of days ashore. I got a wife I'm crazy about. I coulda been a mate on the tug by this time and be making more money than I do here on the dock. But we talked it over soon after we were married and decided it didn't make sense as a way to live. Here on shore I get home every night." There was a long pause, and then he added, "Money ain't everything, you know."

My watercolor came along fairly well. As I was putting in the accents and finishing touches, the super came back again.

"You really got it," he said admiringly, as we both stood back and took a look at it. "You know, you ought to show that to old Cap Isbrandtsen."

"Why Captain Isbrandtsen?" I asked.

"Hell, that's his ship. I'll bet he'd buy that picture from you. Whoa, wait a minute," he added, "you forgot to put in her name."

I realized it would do no good to argue, so I got out a sharp-pointed knife and started to scratch out in white under the shadow of her bow the square lettering of her name: *Flying Trader.*

"You read about her, haven't you?" the super asked.

"Can't say that I have," I replied as I went on working.

"Sure. The papers have been full of her. She's the ship whose captain has been accused of killing a member of the crew on her last trip. That's the reason she's tied up here now. She'd 'a been at sea by now if the captain weren't in jail and the crew in court testifying."

Of course! It all came back to me. The papers had been full of the story. The trial was making news every day. (The captain was not convicted.)

The super came back, as I was packing up my things, to say good-by. "Say," he insisted with enthusiasm, "you gotta come back next week. The *Flying Cloud* will be in. She's a beauty, biggest and newest in the fleet. This'll be her first trip. She oughta make a swell picture."

"I'll try," I promised.

"If you can't make it next Saturday," he added as we shook hands warmly, "come back any time."

I have never been back, though I still have it on a list of preferred spots to paint. Someday I hope to visit that neighborhood again.

When I got home I matted up the *Flying Trader.* It looked pretty good; so I went one step further and placed it under glass in a temporary (button-back) frame and kept it around for quite a while. It is still matted and filed away in a closet with other watercolors. I get it out once in a while and take another look at it; never without thinking of the super.

My wife and daughter and I were planning our day over the breakfast table one morning in Paris, a few years ago. "This is the afternoon when we have cards to Christian Dior's salon," said my wife. "Would you like to go?"

I shook my head. "If you don't mind, I'll bow out. As a matter of fact, I think I'll do a watercolor."

"There will be beautiful models at Dior's," added my wife, as she eyed me over her cup of coffee.

"Yes, I know. And I'll admit I have a weakness for beautiful models," I acknowledged, "but I haven't had a chance to do a watercolor since we arrived in Paris. Something tells me this is my day."

"What are you going to paint?" she asked.

"Well," I said, considering the question thoughtfully for a moment, "nearly every artist who comes to Paris does a picture of Notre Dame from the left bank of the Seine. I don't know why I should be an exception."

While my family went shopping that morning, I took the underground to a station near the Ile de la Cité, crossed the island to the left bank, and walked slowly eastward, looking back at intervals at the cathedral. The trees, the bookstalls, the bridges, and the people strolling the embankment were all there as they have been painted so many times. A little beyond the Pont de l'Archevêché, I leaned over the parapet and discovered that the riverbank below was rather wide and that there were even a couple of small trees which would throw some additional shade to work in. A stairway led to the embankment close at hand. Notre Dame stood out nicely across the south fork of the Seine, with the Pont de l'Archevêché in the foregound. This, I decided, was it. The ideal spot for which I was looking. I wouldn't have the parapet and the bookstalls in the foreground, but I would have privacy.

Looking behind me across the Quai de la Tournelle for a landmark which would help me locate the spot again when I returned in the afternoon, I found I was diagonally across from the entrance to the Tour d'Argent, the famous restaurant where we had dined, not too happily, on pressed duck only the previous evening. Not being fond of blood-rare fowl, we had enjoyed the view but not the meal.

Shortly after lunch I slipped through the lobby of the Crillon, feeling very conspicuous with my watercolor block and kit of watercolor essentials, and took a taxi to the spot I had chosen on the left bank. When I seated myself on a ledge in the shade of a tree down on the embankment, there wasn't a soul in my immediate vicinity and not another artist anywhere in sight.

I had just finished my pencil outline sketch and was about to start painting, when I looked up to find an elderly woman, small, frail, and with sharp, deeply wrinkled features, standing at my elbow. She had a little sketch pad and pencil in hand and had evidently been seated only a few yards away from me until she came over to see what I was doing.

"Bon soir," I said, trying one of my meager samples of French. There was no answer. She continued to examine my outline drawing.

Evidently she did not approve of it, for she finally took pencil in hand and with little jabbing motions pointed first at my paper and then at the cathedral. At the same time she let out a stream of shrill French which was lost on me for, never having studied French, I can command—and understand—only a few halting phrases. But there was no mistaking the fact that her comment was critical.

"Pardonnez-moi," I interrupted a couple of times; *"je ne comprends pas."* But she didn't seem to understand me any better than I did her.

I shook my head hopelessly, shrugged my shoulders, and smiled. She gave up then, turned abruptly, and walked back to where she had evidently been seated before, about ten yards away. Later in the afternoon she paid me one more visit. Again she was volubly critical, but again she left me puzzled and uncomprehending.

A light shower came up around five o'clock, just as I was about to finish. Raindrops are ruinous to a watercolor, leaving it dappled with spots wherever a drop falls, so I hastily covered my watercolor block, gathered my things together, and jumped for the protection of the nearby tree in whose shadow I had been sitting all afternoon. My little old lady was already there, and, to my surprise, so were three other painters, who had evidently been working in oils, for they were carrying easels and canvas.

They were a young and friendly-looking trio, and we engaged in conversation, for I heard them speak to one another in English. They were a husband and wife and a brother-in-law who lived in the outskirts of London. Evidently traveling very simply, they were enjoying a painting trip in France together and were staying at a little hotel on the left bank. Like myself they were amateurs, but each, in his own way, had done a very nice oil of Notre Dame. They were working on small canvas boards, thus achieving economy of materials and convenience in traveling. Since none of them worked in watercolors, they were keenly interested in comparing what they had achieved in oils with what I had been able to accomplish in another medium.

We tried to draw the little old French woman into the conversation, but she didn't seem interested, and since the English trio spoke no more French than I, it was impossible. I did get one quick look at her pencil sketch when we were all comparing our pictures, and it seemed to me rather amateurish. Perhaps she was a better critic than artist.

The shower passed. My English friends and I parted company, rather reluctantly so far as I was concerned, for I found myself wishing that my itinerary were not quite so compelling and that I could join up with them for another afternoon of painting; a wish they seemed to share sincerely, for they expressed it warmly themselves.

Art, I thought to myself as I taxied back to the Crillon, is an international language, even at the amateur level.

My picture of the cathedral of Notre Dame hangs in our bedroom in our apartment in New York. I find myself examining it quizzically now and then, wondering why the old French lady found such fault with it. It certainly isn't a great watercolor, nor is it even one of my best, but I still cannot see anything so glaringly bad as to justify that torrent of criticism she gave it. Good or bad, I find it a happy reminder of an absorbing and carefree afternoon on the left bank of the Seine.

I have had one possible clue to the criticism of the old Frenchwoman. A friend, looking at my picture of Notre Dame one evening, asked if the slender spire which appeared to rise from the junction of the nave and transept of the cathedral was really part of Notre Dame or was the spire of Sainte-Chapelle, the exquisite medieval structure which

This picture of Notre Dame was painted one afternoon from the left bank of the Seine with the Pont de L'Archevêché in the foreground. Measuring 17 by 13 inches, it has been mounted in a mat with 4 inches of width showing at top and sides and 4½ inches at the bottom. It is framed under glass in a ¾-inch pickled-oak frame. *See Chapter 9.*

stands a block or two to the west of Notre Dame. My old French critic may have thought so too. Actually, however, there is a spire at this point on Notre Dame—I have looked it up since the question was raised—and the delicate spire of Sainte-Chapelle cannot be seen from where my watercolor was done.

It isn't easy to find time to paint watercolors when one is on a rather hurried sightseeing trip, but I did get in three other pictures in the total of a little more than three weeks my family and I had in Europe together. One was in Scotland, and the other two in Switzerland, in and near the charming village of Montreux on Lake Geneva. All carry memories that no postcard picture could duplicate.

Carrying watercolors along has become a habit with me since I stopped playing golf and tennis. Usually one's business trips are too hurried to make it worthwhile, but I have carried my watercolor kit to the Pacific Coast on occasion and have put it to good use on week ends. And when I arranged a brief spring vacation in Southern California in connection with a business trip, as I did on two occasions, I took my watercolors along as a matter of course.

New scenes, new climates, and a relaxed mood whet one's appetite for painting. In recent years I have found the Caribbean particularly rewarding from that standpoint. Two years ago my wife and I spent two weeks in the American Virgin Islands, dividing our time equally between St. Thomas and St. Croix. Last year we took a similar trip but this time spent half our spring holiday on the island of Antigua, in the British West Indies, and the balance at St. Croix again on our way back.

Christiansted, in St. Croix, has impressed me particularly during my two visits there as a stimulating place to paint watercolors. One can count almost invariably on good weather. Blue skies with scudding clouds, swept along by the trade winds, are almost standard pattern there for nine months of the year. And the town of Christiansted itself is a place of great charm. The Danes, from whom we bought the American Virgin Islands in 1917, built to last during the 200 years or more that the islands were in their possession. The architecture of the buildings in Christiansted reflects a particularly nice combination of Mediterranean and Danish influence. For the most part they are built solidly of brick, but brick which has been painted again and again over the years in lovely pastel shades of blues, pinks, greens, and yellows. The streets are narrow and lined in most of the old part of the town by structures built out over the sidewalk with colonnades supported by the characteristically flat Danish arch.

I was painting a street scene in this atmosphere one morning last spring when a man stopped to look over my shoulder. We engaged in conversation, and I learned he was a professional artist down for a few weeks of painting on St. Croix. I asked how he felt about the island as a place to paint.

"One of the most stimulating places I have ever

visited," was his reply. "I find I just can't resist painting in a setting like this."

Frederikstet, at the western end of the island of St. Croix, is a smaller community than Christiansted, but almost equally quaint and charming. Charlotte Amalie on St. Thomas, a more bustling place with much heavier tourist trade—including the visitors who are there to procure a quick and easy divorce—has its virtues also as a place to paint. The island is smaller than St. Croix but the terrain is more mountainous.

I spent a morning in Charlotte Amalie during my visit there, doing a street scene with the mountains rising rugged and dark against the sunlight in the background. It came along rather well and with few interruptions from visitors until suddenly a school up the street let out for the noon hour. I was immediately surrounded by a rising tide of chattering Negro youngsters. They ranged for the most part from about six to ten years of age. I use the word "chattering" advisedly, for, although they were speaking English, they did so with such a broad Danish accent and such a flat rhythmical rush of words that I could only understand snatches of their conversation.

In their eagerness to see what I was doing, the children crowded so close that I hardly had elbowroom and had to ask them to stand back a little; but they kept edging in closer as I went on with my picture. I was engrossed in painting, and their presence didn't bother me even though there was an occasional scuffle for preferred positions behind me on the steps on which I was sitting. During one such scuffle I thought I heard a slight tinkle of glass but thought nothing of it. A moment later I suddenly felt water soaking through the seat of my faded, French-blue, denim slacks and leaped to my feet to find my water bottle had been overturned and that I was sitting in a puddle. The children scattered like a flock of crows and disappeared.

When I had finished my watercolor twenty minutes later, I packed up my things, picked up my watercolor block, and started gingerly back toward the hotel, glancing back over my shoulder at intervals to see whether other pedestrians were aware of my predicament. Proceeding along the less frequented streets, I was tremendously relieved a few minutes later when one of the many taxicabs which are constantly cruising around Charlotte Amalie came along. I flagged it, jumped in quickly, and beat a hasty retreat to my hotel.

Antigua offers a landscape somewhat similar to that of St. Croix. But the picturesqueness of St. John, the principal town on the island, with the exception of certain limited areas, stems from poverty rather than from quaint architectural charm and beauty. A few government buildings and homes owned by English residents or winter colonists are of sturdy construction and of good design, although even the Anglican church which towers above the town on a sharp rise of ground is in a poor state of repair. The British somehow do not seem to have built to last as the Danes did in the Virgin Islands. The natives —the population of Antigua, like most Caribbean islands, is about ninety per cent Negro—live from hand to mouth and have had to build with almost any materials at hand. Many of them have used the discarded remnants of packing boxes, together with a few new, unpainted boards. Rusty corrugated iron is the universal roofing material. Some of the little houses are brightened by faded patches of paint. The weather mellows all these materials and colors into interesting and paintable subjects.

One afternoon in St. John I found my way into a little dead-end street running from the town up the slope toward the wooded rise of ground occupied by the Anglican church. From one side of this street one looked across at a well-kept row of native houses, each rising a little above the other up the hillside. Above and beyond them towered the twin spires of the church, rising above a middle distance of trees and waving palms. I studied the scene rather carefully for a few minutes from one position and another and finally picked a spot that provided good shade and the view I wanted. Getting my things out of the little Morris car I was driving, I set to work on my outline sketch.

A few curious natives, all of them Negroes, stopped to glance over my shoulder, but they were very considerate and even the children didn't crowd too closely around me. Things went fairly well until I noticed the brilliant sunshine had disappeared and looked up to find threatening clouds banking up overhead. The rain came swiftly. I had to throw my things into the car and dive in myself for cover from the downpour. The shower, an unusually heavy one, lasted for nearly an hour. I drove around for a while, waiting for it to subside, but finally gave up and went back to the hotel.

The next afternoon I came back again, this time with a good break on the weather, and set to work once more on my watercolor. Again I had a few visitors, among them a slender young man with rather fine features. He studied what I was doing for quite a while and then said, "I knew you were an artist as soon as I saw you get out of the car here yesterday."

"Is that so?" I asked. "How could you tell?"

"By the way you looked at the houses and the church." He placed the tips of thumbs and forefingers together to illustrate.

Sure enough, I recalled. I had had no finder with me, and in trying to determine how much of the scene to include in my picture, I had improvised a finder, as I sometimes do, by holding my hands up with the tips of thumbs and second fingers together and studying the scene through the resultant frame.

"But how did you know that meant I was an artist?" I asked.

"I do a little painting myself once in a while," he said, "and sometimes I do just what you did."

I looked up with interest. "How did you get started painting? Did you have lessons in school?"

He shook his head. "No, I just picked it up."

Long Island Churchyard

An interesting architectural subject, softened by the surrounding shrubbery and trees and by the casual arrangement of the gravestones. The burial ground was simplified by leaving out many stones, allowing the attention to be focused on the forepoint of the church and on the lovely spire.

It came out then that he had done a picture of the same street but looking downhill over the town and out over the harbor. He was shy about it all but at the same time apparently was hungry to talk to someone about painting. I came to the conclusion I was probably the first person he had ever encountered with whom he held this interest in common. By this time I was really interested and asked if I could see his picture of the street scene. He agreed to show it to me if I would stop by his place a couple of doors up the street.

He went on then. I watched to see where he turned in so that I would know where to find him. An hour later, when I had finished and had packed my things in the car, I walked on up to see him.

His tiny two-room shack, like all the others in the vicinity, had no glass in the windows. When protection was needed, the windows were shuttered. He was working at the window in the little front room. It turned out that he was a sign painter. He told me proudly that he had painted all the street and building signs for the American Air Force base on Antigua. That must have been the heyday of his prosperity, for the base has been dismantled since the war, although the fine runways are still maintained and used as Antigua's airport.

Behind him on a shelf was his painting. He reached back and handed it to me and, resting my elbows on his window sill as I stood outside, I studied it carefully. The picture, which was clearly representational in a simple, almost primitive sort of way, was painted in oils on a plywood board which had once been part of a box or crate. The perspective was good and the scene had been reproduced with fidelity. It suffered, however, from a lack of the bright color indigenous to that area, and I began to realize that his palette had been limited to the blacks, grays, blues, and whites which were the mainstays of his sign painter's kit.

I congratulated him on his picture. His face lighted up with pleasure. I explained that I was not a professional artist but that I got great pleasure out of watercolor painting as a hobby. I found that he, too, derived a thrill of satisfaction from his own efforts.

My new-found Antiguan artist and I parted warm friends. Driving back through the sun-drenched sugar-cane fields to the little British hotel, beautifully located overlooking the Caribbean five or six miles out of town, I found myself thinking there must be some creative spark in nearly everyone. It crops out somehow if it is fanned, even a little, rather than smothered.

I am more and more convinced of this as I think of the conversations I have had with children when they have gathered about as I have been doing a watercolor. I have a stock question I always ask in order to draw them out: "Do you like to paint pictures?"

The answer, whether in Maine or Florida, California or New York, Long Island or Antigua, is almost always "Yes." Perhaps it really isn't a creative instinct. Maybe it is only the attraction of bright color and the fascination of spreading it on white paper, but I choose to believe that it is the reflection of an instinctive desire for creation.

One of the most interesting spots in Antigua from the standpoint of history as well as paintable material is English Harbor, located on the south shore of the island. Admiral Nelson, when in command of the British West Indies fleet, used to bring the fleet in to the small, completely protected harbor for repairs and reprovisioning. The neglected ruins of the dockyard are interesting to examine, and some of them provide fine subject matter for pictures.

In recent years a local group on the island has been raising a fund to maintain Nelson's dockyard, as it has come to be called, in its present condition. A modest fee for admittance is charged at the ancient gateway to the yard, and a courteous old colored man is an excellent and well-informed guide.

The buildings in best state of repair are what is known as Nelson's house—really the house provided for the commander of the fleet when on shore—and the quartermaster's office. The old harbor and dockyard, rich in the romantic atmosphere of the days of sailing vessels, are not without their touch of romance today.

I took a box lunch with me and went over to English Harbor one morning, prepared to spend the day painting. I had just about finished a watercolor of Nelson's house and was beginning to think about the contents of my lunch box, when a young woman emerged from the building and walked toward me on her way to the waterfront, where she had a small sailing vessel tied up at the embankment. She spoke cordially with a clipped English accent and asked if she might see my picture. We chatted briefly, and I learned that she was living on her boat but had preempted a vacant room in Nelson's house—which was vacant and for the most part unfurnished—and was writing a book.

Later I learned from others that this was the same young woman who had started out from England a couple of years ago with her husband in a 26-foot sloop, which was then swamped in a sudden storm. Her husband had been swept overboard and lost. She, miraculously, was washed ashore and lived to write the story of their adventure, which was subsequently published in England. I understand that the book met with some success. With the proceeds she fitted out another boat of about the same dimensions—actually 23 feet long—and set out alone to sail to the British West Indies. This time she was successful, and having brought her little sloop safely into English Harbor, she was again engaged in writing the story of her adventures for publication. *Life* magazine in its issue of August 3, 1953, published an abbreviated version of her story ("The Atlantic and I," by Ann Davison).

English Harbor seemed to attract the venturesome. That afternoon, while I was in the midst of a watercolor of the old and colorful quartermaster's office, an attractive young English couple came by, followed by a three- or four-year-old towheaded boy, whom I had seen playing around the dockyard with a colored nurse. We engaged in conversation, and I learned that they lived on a handsome 42-foot ketch tied up at the dockyard. They told me, as casually as I might refer to a trip from New York to Chicago, that they had sailed across the Atlantic six times in their boat since the end of World War II.

What their permanent home and occupation were, or whether they had any or not, I never found out. But their boat was available at the time for charter for trips to neighboring islands of the Lesser Antilles, an enticing project which I would like someday to undertake. They could sleep four on board in addition to the crew—consisting only of their little family—a crew in which I would have great faith in view of their experience.

Watercolor painting, as I think you can see, is not only an absorbing and satisfying hobby in itself, but every now and then it is a key to modest adventure, an open-sesame to other people's lives, an introduction to interesting human contacts which it would be difficult to establish in any other way.

chapter 9 MATTING, FRAMING, AND HANGING WATERCOLORS

I have mentioned in an earlier chapter the desirability of keeping a few mats on hand. You can get them for about $1.50 each cut to your order at almost any artists' supply store. They should be cut from very heavy rigid white cardboard with an aperture which will overlap the edge of your watercolor paper about a half inch all round. The mat should measure about three inches in width at top and sides and about three and one-half inches across the bottom.

You will use mats in a couple of ways. First, you will want to mat up a picture when you have it almost finished, in order to see what additional accents are needed. With a mat lending contrast to your colors, the weaknesses in the picture seem to stand out more clearly. Second, you will want to keep your finished watercolors mounted in mats as long as you intend to have them out where people will see them. Watercolors never look their best unless they are matted.

I have mentioned only white mats. There is no objection to mats of other colors except that their usefulness is limited. You can mat in them only pictures whose general color scheme is enhanced by, rather than in conflict with, the color of your mat. And even when colored mats are used, a picture frequently benefits by a narrow (half-inch or less) white mat next to the picture itself.

For most watercolors, very simple, narrow wood frames are most suitable. There is a trend, however, particularly for exhibition purposes, to heavier and more elaborate framing. But even so, watercolors are usually framed more simply than oils.

If one goes in for a rather broad or heavy frame, it is almost essential to reduce the width of the mat. Otherwise, frame and mat together combine to overwhelm the picture. At least for one's earlier efforts, I earnestly recommend simple, inexpensive frames of unfinished or pickled wood, for even the simplest frames will prove to be costly by contrast with other watercolor materials and equipment.

One other suggestion: Have your first frames made with button backs. Equipped with such frames, you can change pictures in your frames quickly and easily. Before you have been at this hobby of watercolor painting very long, you will find yourself eager to see your more successful sketches matted and framed under glass. Mats give watercolors a lift, but the addition of framing under glass steps them up once more. Then you really see your pictures as they should look when hung. And as you achieve successful results from time to time and your work improves, you will want to replace some of your earlier and more primitive efforts. That is why button-back frames prove so useful.

In this process of progress and change, by the way, make a practice of saving your old sketches. Save even those which have turned out to be failures. Someday you will find you want to come back to them. With greater mastery of your watercolor medium you will find your old sketches provide good material for new pictures. On rainy week ends when you are compelled to paint indoors, you can go back to the old subjects, and, freed from the compelling dictates of nature which seem so demanding to beginners painting on the scene, you may be able, with a fresh approach and a little imagination, to achieve results which will surprise you. But whether you ever use the subject again or not, they are worth saving as a measure of progress and a source of encouragement.

When it comes to hanging pictures, most people have a tendency to hang them too high. A picture should be hung so that its focal point of interest is at, or just slightly below, the eye level of a person

A grouping of three small watercolors, each in ¾-inch pickled-oak frames and in white mats with 3 inches showing at top and sides and 3½ inches across the bottom. They add a bright touch of color to what would otherwise be a rather drab setting. The picture at the left is by Hilton Leech; the two at the right are by the author.

of average height when he is standing erect. If they are hung any higher, we have to crane our necks to look at them when we are sitting down; and in our homes and offices we usually enjoy studying pictures after we are seated. When you visit the art galleries, particularly for such major shows as that of the American Watercolor Society in New York, you will find that practically all pictures are hung a little below the eye level of the standing observer.

In this illustration the watercolor has been mounted in a cloth-covered mat of 1⅜-inch width top and sides and 2-inch width at the bottom. Note the narrow white border next to the picture. The frame, silver and white, is 2 inches in width. When a frame as heavy as this is used with a relatively small picture, it is customary to use a narrow mat so that frame and mat together will not overwhelm the picture. The watercolor, only part of which is shown above, is a lovely landscape done by Ogden Pleissner. It is one of the author's prized possessions.

chapter 10 LEARNING BY PAINTING

Is this all? Is there nothing more to say? Of course there is, for watercolor painting is a subject with innumerable ramifications and endless possibilities.

But more important to the amateur, the hobbyist, the beginner, than reading all the things that could be said about how to paint watercolors are the lessons he learns from experience. Once you have grasped a few fundamentals your progress in watercolor painting will depend more on how much you paint than on how much you read about how to paint. Most of us learn most rapidly by doing. That holds true of painting as much as it does of anything else.

I still learn something about this fascinating medium every time I paint a picture. True, I supplement what I learn by reading, by studying the work of others, by experimenting as I go along. To do so adds variety and endless interest to this hobby.

So I urge you to get out and paint. If you do, you will find yourself, as you lay this book aside, on the threshold of your own adventures in watercolor painting.

ABOUT THE AUTHOR

Paul Montgomery was born in Macon, Illinois, but his home during most of his youth was in Decatur. A graduate of Millikin University in his home town, he was honored with a degree of Doctor of Business Administration a few years ago and more recently became a member of the Board of Trustees.

While in college, Mr. Montgomery became a part-time reporter on a local newspaper. Most of his business career, however, has been in the advertising and business phases of magazine publishing. He is in charge of domestic magazine publishing operations for the McGraw-Hill Publishing Company, and an officer, director, and member of the executive committee. He lives in New York City.

Mr. Montgomery took up watercolor painting as a hobby twelve or fifteen years ago. He has found it endlessly fascinating, a restful and absorbing avocation. Today he rarely takes a pleasure trip or goes off on a vacation without carrying his watercolor equipment with him.

INDEX